FAST-STARTING
a CAREER *of*
CONSEQUENCE
Workbook

FAST-STARTING
a CAREER *of*
CONSEQUENCE
WORKBOOK

FRED SIEVERT

NASHVILLE

NEW YORK • LONDON • MELBOURNE • VANCOUVER

FAST-STARTING *a* CAREER *of* CONSEQUENCE
WORKBOOK

Published in New York, New York, by Morgan James Publishing. Morgan James is a trademark of Morgan James, LLC. www.MorganJamesPublishing.com

Unless noted otherwise, all Scripture quotations are from the Holy Bible, New International Version®, NIV® Copyright © 1973, 1978, 1984, 2011 by Biblica, Inc.® Used by permission. All rights reserved worldwide.

Scripture quotations marked ESV are from the ESV® Bible (The Holy Bible, English Standard Version®), copyright © 2001 by Crossway Bibles, a publishing ministry of Good News Publishers. Used by permission. All rights reserved.

Scriptures marked KJV are taken from the King James Version (KJV), public domain.

Morgan James BOGO™

A **FREE** ebook edition is available for you or a friend with the purchase of this print book.

CLEARLY SIGN YOUR NAME ABOVE

Instructions to claim your free ebook edition:
1. Visit MorganJamesBOGO.com
2. Sign your name CLEARLY in the space above
3. Complete the form and submit a photo of this entire page
4. You or your friend can download the ebook to your preferred device

ISBN 978-1-63195-535-8 paperback
Library of Congress Control Number:
2021902439

Cover Design by:
Rachel Lopez
www.r2cdesign.com

Author photos by:
Lisa Mancuso-Horn

Morgan James PUBLISHING Builds with... Habitat for Humanity® Peninsula and Greater Williamsburg

Morgan James is a proud partner of Habitat for Humanity Peninsula and Greater Williamsburg. Partners in building since 2006.

Get involved today! Visit
MorganJamesPublishing.com/giving-back

TABLE OF CONTENTS

ACKNOWLEDGMENTS

The support and encouragement of my family and friends, as well as my extensive network of business associates (all too numerous to mention by name) is what inspired me to complete this workbook and the book it is based on in the face of many other pressing priorities.

The book and workbook are the culmination of much work by an entire team of extremely competent individuals who made my work much easier and more enjoyable.

Writer, researcher, and editor Libbye Morris, added significantly to the book's readability and relevance by identifying and succinctly articulating research findings that strengthened the impact of many elements of the book's advice.

Social media expert Becca Ryan maintained and expanded my platform to readers around the globe who will benefit not only from this work but also the numerous daily postings of related and relevant spiritual stories and advice on our website, www.StoriesOfGodsGrace.com.

I must also thank the following readers of the draft manuscript and trusted friends who provided welcomed and extensive constructive criticism of the initial draft manuscript that served to greatly enhance the book's relatability and readability: The Reverend Joanne Swenson; The Reverend William Ritter; The Reverend Rebecca Mincieli; literary agent Greg

Johnson; and fellow executives J. Scott Davison, Larry Barton, Larry Ward, and Steven Darter.

Dena Stahlheber wrote or edited the sample prayers at the end of each chapter.

And finally, I am grateful to all the fine folks at Morgan James Publishing who immediately recognized the value of the combination of spiritual and business advice contained in *Fast-Starting a Career of Consequence*.

Part 1

INTRODUCTION
AS WE BEGIN...

Is it possible to advance within a secular organization as a strong Christian who regularly professes his or her faith? Does it seem unlikely that the president of a Fortune 100 company could achieve that level of success while freely and openly expressing his or her Christianity?

For me, not only was it possible; it was only through my personal relationship with Jesus Christ, my awareness of my God-given spiritual gifts and my reliance on the daily guidance of the Holy Spirit that such career advancement could ever have occurred.

This workbook and the book it's based on are about the symbiotic relationship between faith and career. As Christians, we are happiest and most pleasing to God when we identify our God-given spiritual gifts and then use them in service to the Lord and in pursuit of our chosen careers.

To set the stage for the advice that is given in this workbook, let me explain the genesis of the book it is based on, *Fast-Starting a Career of Consequence: Practical Christ-Centered Advice for Entering or Re-Entering the Workforce.*

Advice to My Daughter Was the Genesis of the Book

The genesis of the book was a question my daughter, Dena, posed to me after she had graduated from college with a degree in French. She found entry-level employment in the marketing department of a large international cosmetics firm. She was essentially languishing in that position, fulfilling marketing orders. She came to me in near desperation and asked, "What can I do to get noticed and distinguish myself from all the other young employees?"

I thought long and hard about how a new employee at my own company might get a fast start and thereby become recognized as someone of high potential. As a result of fully thinking that through, I initially came up with five tips that I shared with Dena. They are reflected in chapters 6 through 10 of the book and workbook.

Dena, who is also a strong Christian, had enormous success after following these tips, remaining true to her faith and applying biblical principles in the workplace. After observing her success, I decided to use the same tips in mentoring young students, family and friends. Later, I used them as the theme of four commencement addresses I delivered at colleges, universities, and even at one high school. The feedback I've received from those who took the advice and acted on it has been overwhelmingly positive and very gratifying to me.

Little did I know at the time that this would result in a spiritual calling that would fulfill my passion of positively impacting lives for Christ through my faith and my business experiences. Writing the book, and now this workbook, has been a perfect way to do exactly that.

After the early successes, I realized that getting noticed in a large organization can be a daunting task that frustrates many recent graduates, as well as older adults who are re-entering the workplace.

Even if they excelled in their undergraduate studies or in their prior assignments, individuals starting in a new position often ask how they can be noticed or be labeled as "high potential" by their new company and management team. So often, they embark on what they believe is an exciting new opportunity, only to find themselves languishing in a low-level administrative role that provides little or no satisfaction.

They often wonder when the career they hoped for would really get launched. Even business school graduates don't often know how they can become noticed by senior management. This can lead to disappointment, frustration, and a feeling that their expensive education never really panned out the way parents, instructors, and friends had claimed.

In my business career, I was involved in recruiting and managing hundreds of individuals entering the workforce with diverse backgrounds, educational credentials, and life experiences. They almost always entered or re-entered the workforce with enthusiasm and high expectations.

Unfortunately, many had previously become disenchanted or discouraged as their hopes and dreams of future fulfillment and success waned. The mundane routine of holding positions in which they felt unnoticed and unappreciated often left them unmotivated. Their daily work experience ultimately morphed into pure drudgery.

This situation exists today for many employees with a variety of skills and expertise. It is true for the highly educated as well as the less educated. It is even true for those with MBA degrees from highly respected business schools.

This realization then led me to think even more about success factors for those who are entering or re-entering the workplace. I added five more important tips to my original list of five. This new list of ten tips, coupled with the all-important adherence to biblical principles, should propel any Christian reader who diligently follows them to a high likelihood of early career success.

About the Christ-Centered Career Advice in the Book and Workbook

I referred earlier to a symbiotic relationship between faith and career. This workbook is structured to leverage that relationship.

Following the introduction to this workbook, Part 2 (chapters 1–5) discusses the application of Biblical principles in the workplace. These chapters will help you create a strong foundation for fulfillment in your career. The principles offered in these chapters will add a spiritual dimension to your career pursuits that will be very edifying and impactful.

Part 3 of this workbook (chapters 6–15) elaborates on practical steps you can take to rapidly gain visibility and early success as you enter the workforce for the first time, move to a new company, or re-enter the workforce after a period of absence. The ten fast-start tips in these chapters are practical strategies you can implement immediately to generate and maintain your excitement and enthusiasm for a job you have just landed—or one you've been in for a while. These tips, based on my own experience as the former president of a Fortune 100 company, can make all the difference as you launch into a new and exciting phase of your vocational experience, linked inextricably to your personal faith.

This workbook will arm you with advice that will enable you to quickly become noticed and recognized as a high-potential employee who is capable and ready for future advancement and expanded levels of responsibility. In the process, your strong personal faith can positively impact the lives of others who watch your ascension to higher levels within the organization.

Here are just a few examples of common situations you may find yourself in as you seek to enter or re-enter the workplace. If any of the following situations sound familiar to you, you will benefit greatly from the tips and related exercises in this workbook:

- As a recent college graduate, you may have chosen an academic major well-aligned with your interests, but you wonder how it can be used in a meaningful role in business that could lead to future success and fulfillment. In this book, you'll find ways to succeed, whatever your college major. It is not uncommon for people to become highly successful in fields unrelated to their areas of concentration during their college years.

- You may be considering a change in your career to a profession or occupation that you feel is a better match for you but might not adequately compensate you for your efforts. Perhaps your passion is in a discipline that typically doesn't compensate well. If you follow the proven fast-start tips in this book that lead to increased responsibilities and management roles, coupled with the application of the Biblical principles in chapters 1 through 5, you can have the best of both worlds: a Christ-centered career that utilizes your spiritual gifts and provides compensation that more than adequately rewards you for your efforts.

- You may be one of those unfortunate millions who either lost their jobs or were placed on furlough during the COVID-19 crisis. Your re-entry into the workforce may be with the same company or with a new company. In either case, it's a perfect time to establish yourself as someone of high potential with a promising future. This book can be a perfect enabler in your workforce re-entry.

- You have decided to re-enter the workplace after several years of child rearing. If so, you are probably anxious about doing so and feel ill-equipped to succeed after years outside the workforce. Perhaps more than others, you need fast-start tips and coping techniques for dealing with the stress and pressure on re-entry.

- If you recently ended your service to our country after a long or even a short stint in the military, you likely enter the workplace with high expectations, but also with a heightened level of trepidation. You may wonder how you'll succeed when so many of your friends and classmates have a head start on you. Equipped with the strength of your faith and the drive, determination, and discipline you undoubtedly learned in the armed forces, you are, in fact, well-prepared to leverage that experience using the fast-start tips in this book to achieve great personal and professional fulfillment.

- If you are a senior pastor, an associate pastor, a youth minister, or even a lay leader in your church, you might be wondering how you can better serve members of your church who are anxious or stressed out over a major life transition like entering or re-entering the workforce. In fact, all the tips in chapters 6 through 15 apply equally to you in your ministry. Just read the titles to those chapters in the table of contents to confirm the applicability of the advice they provide.

In addition to inspiring and motivating you, this workbook will enable you to accomplish the following:

- Apply biblical principles in all dimensions of your life, including the workplace.
- Get noticed in the workplace, even in a low-level starting position in a large organization.
- Develop pertinent skills and knowledge more rapidly than otherwise possible, even without a mentor or participation in a formal training program. As you'll learn in chapter 3, you can think of Jesus as your workplace partner, as I did.
- Become recognized as a high-potential employee with strong strategic capabilities.
- Enter management ranks more rapidly if you aspire to do so and have identified leadership or management among your spiritual gifts.
- Compete effectively for early promotional opportunities across a broad range of functions and responsibilities.
- Track your progress in implementing the actions steps provided.

Every life, including yours, is a journey that is important to God. As such, every life is one in which He will provide guidance, blessings, and unconditional love. This applies not only to your worship experiences and your family life, but also to your career. Each one of us is endowed with a unique combination of spiritual gifts that we should consider foremost in making future vocational and avocational plans and decisions.

About This Workbook

This workbook is meant to be an invaluable current and future resource for you as you implement the fast-start tips and strategies discussed in the chapters of the book by the same title. It is effective when used for self-study or in a group setting.

The key points, action steps, and cautions in this workbook will provide you with a means to track your progress as you enter or re-enter the workforce with the objective of fast-starting a career of consequence. It also will make it easy for you in the future to quickly review the action steps in selected chapters without requiring that you reread the entire book. Also, each of the fifteen chapters in this workbook ends with a sample prayer that provides a way for you to approach God for guidance in effectively implementing and realizing the value of this advice.

Some of the tips or action steps logically should be deferred until you have established yourself in your new job. Where that is the case, it is mentioned in the cautions section at the end of the chapter summary. Some of the caution sections also note other areas in which you need to be cautious about how rapidly or how aggressively you implement some of the recommendations.

I am confident that your future happiness and success in your chosen profession will be greatly enhanced by working through this workbook and embracing many of these suggestions.

As you read this workbook and complete the exercises, may God richly bless you and encourage you to implement its advice enthusiastically as you embark upon this exciting new journey!

Part 2

CHAPTERS 1–5
FIRST THINGS FIRST—
APPLYING BIBLICAL
PRINCIPLES

Chapter 1
IDENTIFY AND USE YOUR SPIRITUAL GIFTS AT WORK

"For just as each of us has one body with many members, and these members do not all have the same function, so in Christ we, though many, form one body, and each member belongs to all the others. We have different gifts, according to the grace given to each of us. If your gift is prophesying, then prophesy in accordance with your faith; if it is serving, then serve; if it is teaching, then teach; if it is to encourage, then give encouragement; if it is giving, then give generously; if it is to lead, do it diligently; if it is to show mercy, do it cheerfully."

Romans 12:4–8

You have a unique combination of spiritual gifts. Discerning what those gifts are and then using them in Christian service will serve as the foundation for your ability to choose a career that will enable you to optimize your potential and to serve God and others.

Start by Identifying Your Spiritual Gifts

If you have already completed a spiritual gifts assessment exercise and discerned your spiritual gifts, then you are already off to a fast start on your pathway to career success. If you have not done so in the past, I strongly encourage you to take the time now to complete the "Spiritual Gifts in the Marketplace" assessment questionnaire in the appendix. It can be quite enlightening. The results will enhance the effectiveness of what you read in the remaining chapters of this workbook.

Once you have completed that assessment and you feel you have a better understanding of your own unique combination of gifts, I can assure you that Jesus is eagerly awaiting your invitation for Him to guide you on your working journey. You can read more about Jesus as a workplace partner in chapter 3.

Whatever your vocational calling is, you can use your spiritual gifts effectively. As you determine how best to use your unique combination of gifts, you can take comfort in knowing that you are serving the Lord in the workplace.

The assessment tool in Appendix A is only a recommended first step in the process of discernment. Once you identify the top several gifts you scored most highly on, think about your own involvement and attitude toward each. Do the activities you undertake in each area give you great satisfaction? Are you good at them? Do people compliment you on your success in those areas? Have you impacted other lives in a positive way through activities associated with those skills? The answers to such questions are likely to narrow your number of discernible and manageable spiritual gifts to three or four.

In my case, it became clear to me that God had given me the gifts of a strong faith, strategic leadership (most often using my financial acumen), and generosity in giving my time and resources.

Apply Your Spiritual Gifts in the Workplace

During my working life and into my retirement years, I used and effectively deployed those gifts in my personal, vocational, and spiritual pursuits. The gifts manifested themselves in ways that were not discernably different as a Christian; as a businessman; or as a friend, father, and husband. I realized that I was not a Christian at times, a businessman at other times, and a father, friend, or husband at still other times. No, I was all these things all the time.

Although that may seem obvious, it was a revelation for me. I could apply my gifts in all aspects of my life because I could not separate my Christianity from my vocation or from my social and family situation. Many Christians overlook that simple but important reality.

Before I came to this revelation while in my late twenties, I felt that worship was a Sunday-only activity and had no role in the workplace. I never prayed at work, and I talked about my faith only with my friends and acquaintances from church.

Does this sound familiar to you? If it does and you are entering the workplace for the first time, coming to this realization will enable you to magnify your impact along all dimensions of your life and accelerate your advancement and success within your chosen career. You will be way ahead of where I was on my Christian journey when I first entered the workplace at age twenty-two.

—————

Here are three key points from chapter 1 of the book *Fast-Starting a Career of Consequence: Practical Christ-Centered Advice for Entering or Re-Entering the Workforce*:

Key Points

1. Each of us has a unique combination of spiritual gifts. Discerning what those gifts are and then using them in Christian service is perhaps the most successful approach to choosing work that will lead to sustainable happiness and fulfillment.

2. Recognizing what your spiritual gifts are will enable you to magnify your impact along all dimensions of your life and accelerate your advancement and success within your chosen career.

3. God presents us with opportunities to use those gifts in ways that may not be immediately obvious to us. We need to seize those opportunities and respond to God's calling.

Action Steps

1. Complete the "Spiritual Gifts in the Workplace" assessment questionnaire in the appendix to identify the top six or seven spiritual gifts on which you scored highest. Once you have completed the assessment and calculated your responses according to the instructions, you will know which of the following gifts God has blessed you with:

A = Administration
B = Apostleship
C = Compassion
D = Connecting
E = Creativity
F = Cross-Cultural Ministry
G = Discernment
H = Encouragement
I = Evangelism
J = Faith
K = Giving
L = Hospitality
M = Intercessory Prayer
N = Knowledge
O = Leadership
P = Miracle-Working & Healing
Q = Pastoring
R = Prophecy
S = Service
T = Teaching
U = Tongues & Interpretation
V = Wisdom
W = Worship

2. List your top seven gifts here:

    Spiritual Gift #1: —————————————————

    Spiritual Gift #2: —————————————————

    Spiritual Gift #3: —————————————————

    Spiritual Gift #4: —————————————————

    Spiritual Gift #5: —————————————————

    Spiritual Gift #6: —————————————————

    Spiritual Gift #7: —————————————————

3. Now narrow this list down to the top three or four gifts—not necessarily based on your score, but rather taking into consideration which gifts you think will give you the greatest satisfaction and those that will provide you with the best opportunities to serve the Lord:

    Spiritual Gift #1: —————————————————

    Spiritual Gift #2: —————————————————

    Spiritual Gift #3: —————————————————

    Spiritual Gift #4: —————————————————

4. For each gift you've identified, give thoughtful consideration, and write down a plan for how you can best apply those gifts across the personal, vocational, and spiritual dimensions of your life.

    Example: To help you get started, I will recount an example I gave about my own spiritual gifts in the book. As I explained, strategic leadership is one of the gifts God has given to me. One of the ways I used that gift in service to others was to accept an offer to serve on the Board of Trustees of The American College of Financial Services. I later became the chairman of the Budget and Finance

Committee and then served as chairman of the board in 2006 and 2007. At the time, the college's total assets were dangerously low, at around $15 million. I led an effort to monetize the college's real estate asset by selling the campus and leasing back only the buildings that we absolutely needed. This was a somewhat severe and unpopular action, and we had to convince all other board members to agree to it. We executed the plan at the peak of the market, which provided funds to sustain the college for many years. This move also provided an opportunity to invest the proceeds at the bottom of the equity markets following the financial crisis of 2007–08. That fortuitous timing provided outstanding equity appreciation for several years. The college now has a strong balance sheet, with more than $90 million in total assets. When we sold the property, I am convinced that God was using me (and many others) to solve this existential crisis in a way that now allows the college to impact many hundreds of thousands of lives under a strong and sustainable business model.

5. Now, write below some ways you can use your top four spiritual gifts in service to God and to others in your workplace:

Spiritual Gift #1:—————————————————————————

——

——

——

——

——

——

——

Spiritual Gift #2:————————————————————

——————————————————————————

——————————————————————————

——————————————————————————

——————————————————————————

——————————————————————————

——————————————————————————

Spiritual Gift #3:————————————————————

——————————————————————————

——————————————————————————

——————————————————————————

——————————————————————————

——————————————————————————

——————————————————————————

Spiritual Gift #4:————————————————————

——————————————————————————

——————————————————————————

——————————————————————————

——————————————————————————

——————————————————————————

——————————————————————————

Caution

Once you identify your spiritual gifts, avoid the temptation to use them primarily for personal gain. Use them in your personal life and in your workplace to contribute to the greater good.

Pray often that the Holy Spirit will guide you and present you with opportunities to use your unique gifts in the workplace effectively. Pray the prayer shown below, which acknowledges the spiritual gifts God has blessed you with. This prayer also asks God for guidance on how to recognize and act on opportunities to use those gifts in your workplace:

Gracious and Loving God:

Guide me in how to bring forth the gifts you've given to me in all aspects of my life, especially my place of work. Show me how to engage with you at work, using what you've given me to praise you and to be an example of your Kingdom of love and grace to those around me. Thank you that I'm the work of your hands, created for good works (Eph. 2:10). Help me live this out in the opportunities you put before me. In the name of Jesus, amen.

Chapter 2

ALWAYS ACT IN CONCERT WITH YOUR VALUES AND BELIEFS

"In everything set them an example by doing what is good. In your teaching show integrity, seriousness and soundness of speech that cannot be condemned, so that those who oppose you may be ashamed because they have nothing bad to say about us."
Titus 2:7–8

People tend to expect companies and their leaders to have, and espouse, specific sets of beliefs and values. In chapter 7, we will discuss the importance of understanding and embracing your company's mission and vision statements. These important documents articulate a company's purpose for existing and aspirations for the future. It's hard to imagine how a company could move forward without a specific set of guidelines to inform decisions.

It is equally important for you, an *individual*, to have a specific set of beliefs and values to guide your decisions. Without knowing the values that define you and your character, you will have no reference point for determining which companies align with your personal values and beliefs and which companies do not.

If you are looking for a new position or attempting to re-enter the workplace, as you begin to interview with various companies, look at their websites and read their value statements to find out what is important to them. Ask questions during your interview. You are interviewing the potential employer, just as its recruiters are interviewing you.

Key Points

1. Just as companies need to establish core values and beliefs to guide their decisions, individuals need to determine their own core values and beliefs.

2. It is important to determine, and be able to articulate, what your core values are. They define what is important to you, what you will not tolerate, and who you are. Your values also allow you to be constantly mindful of the need for you to maintain your moral compass, foster greater self-awareness, and give you criteria and standards for decision making and for assessing your own performance to see how consistent it is with your company's established beliefs and values.

3. Make sure your core beliefs reflect and align with your Christian beliefs.

4. Most employers tend to value "soft skills"—personality traits—such as a strong work ethic, a positive attitude, honesty and integrity, a motivation to learn, and professionalism.

5. Unethical behavior in the workplace has become more commonplace as pressures build for individuals to achieve aggressive goals. Following your own core values will strengthen your resolve to refrain from taking any unethical or immoral actions.

Action Steps

1. If you have never done so, identify and articulate your own set of core values, and make sure they align with Christian principles. To help you get started, here are two examples of core value statements. One is a corporate statement of Hobby Lobby, and the other is an individual Christian statement of beliefs as embodied in my favorite version of the often-quoted Apostle's Creed:

Example #1: Hobby Lobby is known as a Christian company that abides by Christian principles consistently. Here is the company's core values statement:[1]

From the beginning, the company's core values have formed a foundation to guide decision making, establish the corporate culture and determine how business is conducted. Hobby Lobby's values include:

- Honoring the Lord in all we do by operating in a manner consistent with Biblical principles
- Offering customers exceptional selection and value
- Serving our employees and their families by establishing a work environment and company policies that build character, strengthen individuals and nurture families
- Providing a return on the family's investment, sharing the Lord's blessings with our employees and investing in our community

---

Example #2: The Apostles' Creed:

I believe in God, the Father Almighty, Maker of heaven and earth, and in Jesus Christ, His Only Son, our Lord, who was conceived by the Holy Spirit, born of the virgin Mary, suffered under Pontius Pilate, was crucified, died, and was buried; on the third day, He rose from the dead; He ascended into heaven, and is seated at the right hand of God the Father Almighty; from there He shall come to judge the living and the dead. I believe in the Holy Spirit, the holy catholic church, the communion of saints, the forgiveness of sins, the resurrection of the body, and the life everlasting. Amen.[2]

Each employer is different, but there are some common characteristics that company leaders consider valuable in new hires. According to one career-advice website, the top five values that employers look for are a strong work ethic, a positive attitude, honesty and integrity, a motivation to learn, and professionalism.[3]

If you want to come up with a simpler set of values, here are just a few of many examples of core personal values you can find by Googling "personal values."

- Compassion
- Excellence
- Faith
- Forgiveness
- Generosity
- Grace
- Gratitude
- Harmony
- Honesty
- Integrity
- Kindness
- Loyalty
- Patience
- Personal development
- Relationship building
- Respect for others
- Self-respect
- Wisdom

Now that you've had a chance to read some examples, write below what you believe and the personal core values you wish to adopt as your own:

_____

_____

_____

_____

_____

_____

_____

_____

Caution

If you are encouraged to engage in activities that are against your personal values and beliefs, take a stand. Pray for guidance. Seek out the counsel and support of other Christians. Talk with someone at work whom you trust. Know your legal rights. In some situations, the only solution is to leave the job. But it would be better to stand up for your principles and lose your job than to succumb to corporate greed and immorality and weaken your bond with your Lord and Savior, Jesus Christ.

Prayer

Call on the Holy Spirit to guide you to always act in concert with your personal values and beliefs. Ask the Lord to help you overcome even the slightest temptation to engage in wrongdoing:

Gracious and Loving God:

You knew me before I was born; you know everything about me (Ps. 139:1–4). Guide me in the core beliefs and values from your Word that you want me to live by and that I can use to lead by example. Let these values from your Word be the light unto my path (Ps. 119:105) as I navigate difficult situations or face temptation to partner with things of this world. In the name of Jesus, amen.

Chapter 3

JESUS AS A WORKPLACE PARTNER

"Come to me, all you who are weary and burdened, and I will give you rest. Take my yoke upon you and learn from me, for I am gentle and humble in heart, and you will find rest for your souls. For my yoke is easy and my burden is light."

Matthew 11:28–30

"Do not be yoked together with unbelievers. For what do righteousness and wickedness have in common? Or what fellowship can light have with darkness?"

2 Corinthians 6:14

Jesus is the best possible and most powerful imaginable workplace partner or companion. We must always remember, however, that we are not on an equal level with Jesus; no humans are. We strive to serve Him, to live in a way that will please Him, and to use our spiritual Gifts to honor and glorify Him.

Jesus is not only your Lord and Savior, but He also can be a powerful and helpful workplace partner through the advice and guidance of the Holy Spirit. On a daily basis, share your workplace challenges and issues with Him, and ask for guidance.

24

Key Points

1. As Christians, we all know how important it is to live according to Christian principles, and to put our trust in Jesus Christ, as we navigate our personal lives, relationships, and difficulties. It might not seem as obvious to rely on our faith as we navigate our careers. But it is important to do so. Our careers represent a significant part of our lives and our identities. Considering Jesus as a workplace partner can make work-related decisions and challenges much easier.

2. Throughout my career, I felt Jesus was an omnipotent, omniscient, omnipresent workplace partner. I love the imagery of being yoked to Jesus (as noted in Matthew 11:28–30, shown above), while tackling the heavy lifting of difficult issues and challenges. In sharp contrast to that imagery is the warning from the Apostle Paul in 2 Corinthians 6:14 to avoid being yoked to, or partnering with, unbelievers. This doesn't mean we can't engage or work with others (even non-believers)—and as a result, have a positive influence on them—but as Christians, our values have to come from being yoked to Jesus.

3. As Christians, we rely on the Holy Spirit to help us become more and more like Jesus. It is a lifelong journey that probably will never be fully achieved. But if you are mindful of the goal and you are constantly striving to achieve it, your happiness and success will essentially be assured.

4. In what the Bible says and what Jesus Himself says, we have a model for success in any endeavors we pursue. Be intentionally and constantly mindful of the fact that the model applies to all aspects of your life—especially in the workplace, where you spend most of your waking hours.

5. If you ultimately aspire to management and/or leadership positions, please review Appendix B in the book Fast-Starting a Career of Consequence, titled "What You Can Learn from the Bible and Jesus about Leading and Managing." It describes Jesus's managerial and leadership traits and Scriptures that reference those traits.

Action Steps

1. Think of the powerful imagery of being yoked to Jesus (as noted in Matthew 11:28–30, shown at the beginning of this chapter) while tackling the heavy lifting of difficult issues and challenges.

    Identify an example of a significant challenge you recently faced that you relied on Jesus to help you solve:

    _____

    _____

    _____

2. Identify an example of a significant challenge you recently faced that you *did not* rely on Jesus to help you solve:

    _____

    _____

    _____

    In that situation, how could you have benefited from having Jesus as a partner?

    _____

    _____

    _____

3. Read what the Bible says about work. Throughout the Old Testament and the New Testament, there are numerous scriptural references to the importance of work and conducting it in a responsible, trustworthy, and reliable way. Here are some passages to read, either in your Bible or in chapter 3 of the book *Fast-Starting a Career of Consequence*:

    -   Genesis 2:15
    -   Psalm 128:2

- John 13:3–5
- Colossians 3:23–24
- 1 Peter 4:10

Does one of these verses resonate strongly with you? Which one, and why?

_____

_____

_____

_____

_____

4. Learn from Jesus. His behaviors and words can set an example for you and provide comfort to you throughout your career. Understanding the ways in which Jesus conducted Himself while in human form are worthy of emulation. They can greatly impact your future. Here are some passages to read, either in your Bible or in chapter 3 of the book *Fast-Starting a Career of Consequence*:

- Mark 8:36
- Matthew 6:33
- Matthew 25:23
- Mark 11:24
- Luke 16:10

Does one of these verses resonate strongly with you? Which one, and why?

_____

_____

_____

_____

5. Take great comfort in the promises He made to us in the following representative Scriptures from the firsthand witnesses and authors of the four Gospels:

- Jesus assures us of his dominion and his eternal presence: Matthew 28:18–20
- Jesus tells us that with God, all things are possible: Mark 10:27
- Jesus assures us of the power of prayer: Luke 11:9–10
- Jesus promised that the Holy Spirit will be given to those who keep His commands: John 14:15–16
- Your primary objective in the workplace should be to serve the Lord, not to amass wealth: Mark 8:36
- If your priorities are well-aligned with Jesus's teachings, you will be rewarded: Matthew 6:33
- As you face difficult issues and challenges in the workplace, rely on faith: Matthew 17:20
- Jesus wants to see you thrive and grow: Matthew 25:23
- Don't restrict your prayer life only to Sundays or only to your house of worship. Pray often at work: Mark 11:24
- Earn trust through honesty and integrity: Luke 16:10

6. To consider Jesus a business partner as you enter or re-enter the workforce, remember what the Apostle Paul said are the fruits of the spirit in his letter to the Galatians:

"But the fruit of the Spirit is love, joy, peace, forbearance, kindness, goodness, faithfulness, gentleness and self-control."
Galatians 5:22–23

7. Be intentionally and constantly mindful of the fact that the model applies to all aspects of your life—especially in the workplace, where you spend most of your waking hours. List four ways you can demonstrate these fruits of the spirit in your workplace:

A. _____

B. _____

C. _____

D. _____

Caution

As you strive to succeed in your career, remember your primary objective: to serve the Lord, not to amass wealth.

Prayer

Call on the Holy Spirit to guide you in emulating Jesus as you share your unique gifts in the workplace. Ask the Lord to help you make decisions that align with Jesus's teachings and to rely on Him as a workplace partner:

Gracious and Loving God:

They called you "Rabbi" or "teacher" (John 3:2) because you spoke and walked in truth and wisdom for all to learn through your demonstration of mercy and grace. Please teach me to be like you, using the unique gifts you have given me to benefit your Kingdom. Illuminate your Word to guide me in my decisions and remind me to look to you first in all things. In the name of Jesus, amen.

Chapter 4

PRAY OFTEN FOR GUIDANCE FROM THE HOLY SPIRIT

"And I will ask the Father, and he will give you another advocate to help you and be with you forever—the Spirit of truth. The world cannot accept him, because it neither sees him nor knows him. But you know him, for he lives with you and will be in you."
John 14:16–17

As Christians, nothing is more central to our beliefs and our ability to emulate and follow Jesus than the concept of the Holy Trinity and the importance of the Holy Spirit, who dwells within us.

In business, we often need to make difficult decisions, and we stress about the right thing to do. Even in cases in which an ethical response is called for, the best decision is not always easily discernible. There often seem to be nuanced considerations.

Making the "right" decision often becomes a difficult task, and then communicating a decision can be equally difficult but no less important. The most effective and convincing words don't always flow naturally from our lips.

As indicated in John 14, the Father will give you an advocate, and you need to trust in that assurance. I hope you will find, as I have, that prayer and the guidance of the Holy Spirit are essential elements of your successful entry or re-entry into the workplace.

Prayer Enhances Our Well-Being

Christians, as well as followers of other religions, understand the benefits of prayer in strengthening their spiritual well-being and connection to God. But research shows that prayer benefits our mental, emotional, and physical health as well. Studies have shown a direct relationship between spirituality and positive health outcomes, including those related to mortality, physical illness, mental illness, health-related quality of life, and the ability to cope with illness, including terminal illness.

The benefits of prayer are so significant, in fact, that there is an entire new field of science devoted to understanding the types of changes that take place in our brains when we engage in religious experiences or practices. It's called *neurotheology*, or the neuroscience of religion.

At the forefront of this research is Andrew Newberg, MD, a neuroscientist at Thomas Jefferson University in Philadelphia. He says, "When prayer elicits feelings of love and compassion, there is a release of serotonin and dopamine." He explains that both of these neurotransmitters play a role in how you feel. Serotonin has a direct impact on your mood, and not having enough serotonin has been linked to depression. Dopamine, on the other hand, is associated with reward and motivation. Newberg and his colleagues found that in following a retreat centered on prayer and meditation, people experienced beneficial, long-term changes in their dopamine and serotonin levels. He believes that both prayer and meditation can result in permanent changes in the brain regarding these neurochemicals.[4]

There is evidence that the benefits associated with praying are greater if you believe God is a loving, caring Creator, as opposed to viewing God as a strict, angry disciplinarian.

Praying for Others Benefits Us, Too

I have kept a daily prayer list for many years. Every morning, I go through the list and pray individually for all those on the list. The list is a diverse collection of people ranging from immediate family members to colleagues from work to national and local leaders, and even strangers I may have met only once but who shared their prayer needs with me.

It is especially important to pray for people you interact with at work. Work-related relationships are often strained and difficult. But, in addition to praying for improvement in those relationships, pray for nonwork-related personal struggles or illnesses you might learn about that your colleagues in the workplace are facing.

Telling coworkers that you are praying for them or for their family members is perhaps one of the easiest ways to share your faith while letting them know you care. It is exceptionally gratifying when you learn that those prayers were answered. I have much experience in doing this at work. Some of my strongest work-related relationships flourished after committing time in prayer in support of coworkers' needs.

"And I will do whatever you ask in my name, so that the Father may be glorified in the Son. You may ask me for anything in my name, and I will do it."

John 14:13–14

Key Points

1. Prayer is essential, not only in your personal worship, but also in the workplace and in all dimensions of your life.

2. Jesus spoke specifically of the Holy Spirit in these Gospel verses:
   - Matthew 28:19–20
   - Mark 13:11,
   - Luke 24:49
   - John 14:15–17

3. The writings of the Apostle Paul are also dense with references to the Holy Spirit. Here are some examples:

- 1 Thessalonians 4:8
- Galatians 4:6–8
- Philippians 1:19
- 1 Corinthians 2:10–14
- 2 Corinthians 5:5
- Romans 5:3–5

4. In chapter 4 of the book this workbook is based on, I have mentioned several research studies that show how beneficial prayer is to our well-being. Here are some examples of what research says about prayer:
    - Prayer can benefit our mental, emotional, and physical health.
    - Prayer can help alleviate anxiety, uncertainty, and worry.
    - Benefits of prayer are greater if you believe God is a loving, caring Creator, as opposed to a strict, angry disciplinarian.
    - Prayer inspires forgiveness and reduces anger and aggression.
5. You will find praying for guidance to be an essential Bible-based practice throughout your entire career.

Action Steps

1. Read what Jesus said about prayer. Here are some passages to read, either in your Bible or in chapter 3 of the book *Fast-Starting a Career of Consequence*:
    - Matthew 5:43–44
    - Matthew 18:19–20
    - Mark 11:24–25
    - John 14:13–14

    From these passages, what is particularly reassuring to you, and why?

    _____

    _____

2. If you do not engage in regular prayer already, begin doing so. Make a habit of praying often, both at home and in the workplace. Keep a daily prayer list that you attend to at a designated time every day, and be sure to make note of prayers from the list that have been answered. As indicated in the book, pray short, silent prayers at work—even during critical meetings at which major decisions are made, those prayers are heard, and often answered.

    In what ways has regular prayer helped you?

    _____

    _____

    _____

    _____

3. In the book, I also note what research says about the benefits you can derive from intercessional prayer for others. I have maintained a prayer list for my entire adult life, and I am always in awe about the amazing ways that God answers prayers I make on behalf of people I know. If you do not do so already, begin praying for others. Start a list right now of those people you know who are in desperate need of prayer. Lift them up in. prayer, starting today, and continue to add to that list over time. List here those who will initially be on your list for intercessional prayers.

    A. _____

    B. _____

    C. _____

    D. _____

    E. _____

Cautions

1. Your practice of praying in the workplace can and should be done often, but that doesn't mean it needs to be overt and outwardly evident to all around you. I typically prayed ten to fifteen times daily at work. Many times, I prayed silently while attending a difficult meeting.

2. Sharing our faith in Christ is vitally important. However, early in your career, I would caution you about being too aggressive in this regard. Be patient, and rely on the Holy Spirit to provide you with appropriate opportunities to share your faith.

Prayer

Call on the Holy Spirit to help you build the habit of praying often, wherever you are. Ask the Lord to remind you to call on Him first, before struggling to decide which path to take in each situation:

Gracious and Loving God:

Thank you that you made prayer a way for us to speak to and hear from you. Strengthen my relationship with you out of love and devotion as my trusted guide, teacher, friend, and savior. Let your Holy Spirit remind me and show me that you are ever-present in me, hearing and responding to my prayers (1 John 5:14–15). Transform my heart to be more like yours, ever seeking you for who you are, not out of duty or obligation. In the name of Jesus, amen.

Chapter 5

APPLY THE GOLDEN RULE WITH EMPLOYEES AND CUSTOMERS

"Do onto others as you would have them do onto you."
Luke 6:31

Almost all of us were aware, as children, of the Golden Rule. The words "do unto others as you would have them do unto you" were spoken by Jesus Himself in the books of Matthew and Luke.

But many times, once we become adults, we forget about the Golden Rule and rarely apply it in the business world. It's a Bible-based principle that, if adhered to in the business world, will serve employees and customers well. It can even create competitive advantage for companies and career-advancement opportunities for employees. My focus in this workbook is how your awareness and application of this principle can enhance your entry or re-entry into the workplace.

In this chapter, we explore ways to treat those in our workplaces as we would like to be treated ourselves.

Recent Business Practices Often Ignore the Principle

Increasingly, more and more companies are using artificial intelligence, robotics, big data analytics, online promotions, and other types of automation to expand their market penetration, and thus their profits and growth. But many times, a dependence on automation diminishes the quality of care companies provide to employees and service they provide to customers.

In this high-tech environment, the Golden Rule is more relevant than ever in defining how employers should treat their employees and customers. The "Golden Rule" is the adage that became assigned to the biblical principle of treating others as you would want to be treated yourself.

With constant assaults on our privacy and companies' reliance on machines and voice software, it is more important than ever to gain sustainable competitive advantage (the essential goal of *strategy*) through strong and personal customer service. Millions of consumers are turned off by some of today's "creative" but impersonal and intrusive marketing and servicing techniques. By facing and addressing this reality, your company's leaders can help their bottom line greatly by making a concerted effort to follow the biblical principle.

Entering a company as a new employee, initially you won't have decision-making authority to change much of what you read about in this chapter. However, even as a new employee you can distinguish yourself by demonstrating an awareness of these issues and you can begin to position yourself for possible management or leadership roles in the future.

In this chapter, I suggest a number of action steps. You can apply them in stages, as your knowledge evolves over time on issues relating to the application of the Golden Rule.

Today's Lack of Personalized Customer Service Presents an Opportunity

Now that technology is an integral part of the business landscape, sometimes employees' efforts to abide by the Golden Rule are compromised.

Heavily automated processes, which many companies install to reduce operating costs and increase efficiency, can interfere with the human interaction that enhances customers' overall experience with companies. For example, studies have shown that many customers dislike international call centers and robocalls.

It is remarkable to reflect on the changes that have occurred over just the past few decades. These changes demonstrate a strong and rapid movement away from the wisdom of the Golden Rule articulated so succinctly in the Bible almost two thousand years ago.

This situation creates an opportunity for you, over time, to begin to reverse the trend and provide meaningful and constructive input to the management of your own company. However, I would advise you to proceed cautiously and pray for guidance from the Holy Spirit as you begin to make observations and communicate your suggestions to those who can ultimately effect change.

The one universal area for meaningful and sustainable competitive advantage is in the company's relationship with its customers and the services it provides to them.

The Golden Rule as a Biblical Principle

In this age of impersonal communications, technological advancements, and fewer direct human interactions than historically has been the case, the Golden Rule is even more relevant and more important than when it was articulated by Jesus, as told in the Gospels of Luke and Matthew.

At work, at home, and in every interaction we have with others, the Golden Rule is a simple and abiding guideline that encourages us to treat others well, show compassion, and "love thy neighbor as yourself"—in essence, the Christian tenet of emulating Jesus in every way.

Key Points

1. In this age of impersonal communications, technological advancements, and fewer direct human interactions than historically have been the case, the Golden Rule is even more relevant and more important than when it was first articulated in the Gospels of Luke and Matthew.

2. The one universal issue and area for meaningful and sustainable competitive advantage is in your company's relationship with its customers and the services it provides to them.

3. The current, often negative, state of customer and employee relations creates an opportunity for you, over time, to begin to reverse recent trends and provide meaningful and constructive input to the management of your own company.

4. Entering a company as a new employee, initially you probably won't have decision-making authority to change much of what you read about in chapter 5 of the book. However, even as a new employee, you can distinguish yourself by demonstrating an awareness of these issues. Such insights can begin to position you for possible management or leadership roles in the future.

5. When you come across communications or practices that you feel compelled to communicate to someone, it is best to pray about it first and then proceed cautiously and wisely. Any indication of arrogance, perceived superior intellect, or judgment on the part of an employee who is new to the company can be a major career blocker. Unless your role in the company is directly related to assessing and improving customer relations or services, initially you should view your observations as early fact-finding. You will get opportunities to roll out your suggestions over time, as your career advances.

6. The one universal issue and area for meaningful and sustainable competitive advantage is in the company's relationship with its customers and the services it provides to them. In my opinion, the revolution in online and phone technology, in many ways, has been regressive rather than progressive. This is yet another case in which the simplicity of biblical principles is timeless and overrides technological improvements. The trend toward technology-driven customer service creates an enormous opportunity for you and your company.

Action Steps

1. Your best opportunity to observe customer interactions and communicate ideas for improvement will come only after

you become a customer yourself. Purchase some of your own company's products and then, as a customer, interact with the customer service department, either by telephone or online. Read all its communications, whether you received them in the mail, by email, or via the internet. Below, note who you spoke with, what types of communications you received, and your observations from those interactions, both good and bad. Keeping these notes will enable you to come back and review this information later:

Whom You Spoke With	The Outcome	Observations

2. Obtain valuable customer feedback from your company's distributors. No matter what type of products or services your company is offering, someone sells them. Distributors of your products are on the front lines and closest to the customer. As a result, they can provide you with the best insights regarding how customers are treated by, and tend to interface with, the company. If necessary, ask your direct supervisor how you can be introduced to one or more of the company's distributors. Just asking that question will likely impress your boss. Note below which distributors you spoke with on which dates, and summarize key information you gathered:

Distributors You Spoke With	Date(s)	Key Observations

3. Develop the habit of thoughtfully observing human interactions among employees within your company. Here are a few examples of common employee-to-employee or company-to-employee internal interactions. As you observe these interactions in your job, note any situations here that are not up to par with your company's ideal standards:

Type of Interaction	Observations and Lessons Learned
A face-to-face meeting with a superior, a peer, or a subordinate	
An email, voicemail, or text communication	
A corporatewide communication to all employees	
A performance review by your immediate supervisor	
A verbal confrontation in a staff meeting	
A public reprimand of you or someone else	
Gossip or criticism of others in the workplace	

4. Identify an example of an interaction that causes you to experience some level of discomfort. Describe the situation, and answer the following questions. Be mindful of the Golden Rule as you consider your answers.

- **Situation:**

    Describe what you observed. Is there anything about this experience that could have been handled in a more effective way to generate the hoped-for reaction or response? If so, what?

    _____

    _____

    _____

    _____

    If you were the person involved in delivering such a communication, how would you have handled it differently?

    _____

    _____

    _____

    _____

    If you were the person on the receiving end, how would you have preferred to be treated?

    _____

    _____

    _____

    _____

Is this situation serious enough that you felt compelled to comment on it or intervene? If so, what would be the most tactful and effective way to communicate your concerns?

_____

_____

_____

_____

_____

5. Observe the processes that people follow throughout your company. Which ones, in your opinion, are so technology-based that they interfere with or prevent sincere face-to-face interactions and personal communications? Write below which processes seem to be heavy on technology and light on personal interaction. Beside each one, write your suggestion for improving the process so it still makes use of technology but also enhances customer interactions:

Processes That Rely Too Much on Technology	Your Suggestions for Increasing the Personal Interactions in This Process

Cautions

1. Most of the advice given in this workbook can be implemented early in your tenure with a new company and on a relatively aggressive timetable. But in the case of communicating your critique of interactions with the company's employees and customers, caution is the better part of valor.

2. Early in your career or in a new job, it is wise to proceed cautiously. You don't want to appear arrogant or risk antagonizing someone who implemented technological enhancements in a cost-saving exercise.

3. As your career advances and you begin to manage others, you will certainly be a more effective coach or mentor after learning what you have learned from the above practices.

Prayer

As you make these observations, pray for guidance from the Holy Spirit for discernment about communicating your suggestions to those who can ultimately effect change. Pray also that the Lord, through the Holy Spirit, will provide you with opportunities to present your findings—and the wisdom to do so tactfully and at the most appropriate time. Call on the Holy Spirit to guide you in following the Golden Rule—with clients, customers, and fellow team members:

Gracious and Loving God:

Thank you for how you guide and teach us. I pray for a servant's heart to steward whatever wisdom or knowledge you would share with me about this company. I ask for your divine timing and help to discern whom to share this with for your glory. I ask that you would protect me from pride or selfish ambition (Rom. 12:3) as I grow in my understanding of what this organization can do to provide superior services and experiences for its clients, customers, and employees. In the name of Jesus, amen.

Part 3

CHAPTERS 6–15
TEN PROVEN FAST-START TIPS

Chapter 6

DEMONSTRATE COMMITMENT

"Whatever you do, work at it with all your heart, as working for the Lord, not for human masters."

Colossians 3:23

In the chapters that follow, I offer many practical tips and strategies for fast-starting your career as a Christian. But no strategy rivals clearly demonstrating commitment to your company by some simple actions and behaviors.

If you have identified your spiritual gifts as discussed in chapter 1, you will have positioned yourself to make intelligent decisions on how to demonstrate your commitment by doing so in concert with your understanding of your own unique combination of spiritual strengths and gifts.

It's Obvious Who Is Committed and Who Is Not

One of the most noticeable ways to demonstrate commitment to a company is to arrive at work early and leave late.

To understand the typical behavior of many employees, all you have to do is observe how many people enter a company in the few minutes before the workday begins and see how many leave as soon as, or just minutes after, the workday ends. At the beginning of the workday, you are most likely to observe a rush at the official start of the day, with many stragglers coming in late. At the end of the workday, if it's a large company, you will probably witness a near stampede of individuals rushing out the doors at or before the designated close of business.

While it may be difficult for high-ranking executives of the company to notice which employees are coming in precisely at the opening of business, or leaving precisely at the close of business, it is much easier to spot those who are at their workstations thirty minutes before the official workday begins and those who stay well beyond the official closing time. Typically, top executives are on the job early and leave late—so your presence will be noticed by those whom you hope will notice. This is a simple way to demonstrate your commitment, and it will be well worth the additional investment of your time.

The Importance of a Positive Attitude

When you are new to an organization or department, people are getting to know what type of person you are. It is critical to maintain a positive attitude, even when—especially when—facing a difficult situation. If you do this, you will gain a reputation for maintaining your composure and professionalism, even when feeling pressured.

I fondly remember a dozen or more people I interacted with regularly during my career who always lifted my spirits with their own positive attitudes. The joy they derived from coming to work and interacting with others at all levels was infectious. In particular, their uncanny ability to agreeably disagree with others in a confrontation that could otherwise get nasty was remarkable. I tried hard to emulate such behaviors, and I recommend that you do the same.

Setting a Standard for Others to Follow

Much has been written about mission-driven organizations, but not as much about mission-driven employees. You can set a standard that few others will naturally exhibit by demonstrating your commitment to your company; being vocal about the value of what it does; and expressing your joy in, and gratitude for, being a part of it.

You've heard it said that if you follow your passion, you will never work a day in your life. I have found that to be absolutely true. But it is also true that *demonstrating* your passion can exponentially increase your impact on the organization and that will be noticed and rewarded.

Key Points

1. One of the best strategies for getting a fast start in your career is to demonstrate clearly your commitment to your company.

2. Few employees know their companies' mission statements. Learning, understanding, and promoting your company's mission statement will distinguish you from most of your peers.

3. CEOs and managers typically place a high value on work ethic. You can demonstrate a strong work ethic by your actions, such as seeking out more work.

4. Being visible and meeting as many people as you can throughout your organization will help you get noticed.

5. A positive attitude is a must, especially when circumstances are not ideal. By maintaining a positive attitude even in the midst of turmoil, you will establish yourself as someone with leadership potential.

Action Steps

1. Demonstrate your commitment to your company by arriving at work early and leaving late.

   How much added time are you willing to commit to per day or per week?

   _____

   _____

   For Action Steps #2 through #5 below, if you have not yet landed a job, complete these exercises for the company you are most interested in working for.

2. Know the ways in which your work effort is supporting that mission. In appropriate circumstances, such as during your annual performance review, state the ways in which your specific role and responsibilities support your company's mission. Write them below:

_____

_____

_____

_____

3. Be vocal about the value of what your company does, as well as your joy in, and gratitude for, being a part of it. Write a short expression of that joy and gratitude:

_____

_____

_____

_____

4. Demonstrate a strong work ethic by taking the following actions:
    *   Complete projects on time and within budget.
    *   Focus on execution and completion of your daily work assignments.
    *   Take on difficult tasks with enthusiasm.
    *   Deliver on your promises.
    *   Always act with integrity, honesty, and accountability.
    *   Demonstrate elements of your work ethic that also convey your values—the ethics part of the expression "work ethic."

5. Are any of the above actions particularly difficult for you? If so, which ones and how do you plan to work on them?

_____

_____

_____

6. Seek out more work. Here are some ways to get noticed in this area:
   - Be willing and eager to do more for the company.
   - Accomplish everything asked of you in excellent and timely fashion but also make it clear that you are willing to do, and contribute, more.
   - Express your commitment, not only as a willingness to help the company succeed, but also as a way for you to learn more about the business and support its mission.

7. What skills do you have that might be useful outside of your normal job responsibilities?

_____

_____

_____

8. Be visible. To increase your visibility, consider doing the following:
   - Help plan, and/or participate in, company and departmental functions and celebrations.
   - Be a part of company-sponsored volunteer activities.
   - Take lunch and coffee breaks in the company cafeteria, and try to meet employees from other departments whom you haven't previously met.
   - Occasionally show up at the office for an hour or two on the weekend. You'll almost certainly be noticed as you run into other similarly committed employees.

- Participate in developmental courses or training offered by your company.
- If yours is a publicly traded company, attend the annual shareholder meeting.

9. To what extent are you being as visible as possible? Write below some ways in which you can make yourself more visible in an appropriate way:

_____

_____

_____

_____

Cautions

1. Never let complacency rob you of your drive to excel. Even if you think no one notices you and what you're doing, you can rest assured that people do notice.

2. Avoid the temptation to ease up on your efforts once you get comfortable in your new position. Continue to follow and employ the recommendations in this book, and over time, you will distinguish yourself from those around you in a significant way.

Prayer

Pray that the Holy Spirit will make you aware of opportunities to demonstrate your commitment in ways that will be valuable to your team and company. Pray for strength to always strive to demonstrate humility and empathy.

Gracious and Loving God:

Please instill in me a heart for the people I work with. Help me live out your values and those of the company, demonstrating my commitment to you while being of service to my team and those around me. I ask for a spirit of excellence, doing all that is put before me for your glory, not my own (1 Corin. 10:31). Let my actions and participation demonstrate my commitment to you and to my place of work. In the name of Jesus, amen.

Chapter 7

UNDERSTAND AND EMBRACE THE COMPANY'S VISION AND MISSION

"Where there is no vision, the people perish: but he that keepeth the law, happy is he."

Proverbs 29:18 (KJV)

"The plans of the diligent lead to profit as surely as haste leads to poverty."
Proverbs 21:5

"Many are the plans in a person's heart, but it is the LORD'S purpose that prevails."

Proverbs 19:21

Research shows that the leaders in most American companies understand that they need to produce mission and vision statements to ensure that everyone in the organization is working toward a common goal. As Proverbs 21:5 says, "The plans of the diligent lead to profit."

However, many companies are not doing a good job of communicating these mission and vision statements—or inspiring their teams to understand, agree with, and internalize core values.

The Difference between a Vision Statement and a Mission Statement

It can be confusing to distinguish between a vision statement and a mission statement unless you understand the difference between the two. The Society for Human Resource Management explains the purpose of both statements.[5]

A *vision statement* looks forward and creates a mental image of the ideal state that the organization wishes to achieve. It is inspirational and aspirational and should challenge employees. A vision statement reveals answers to these questions:

- What problem are we seeking to solve?
- Where are we headed?
- If we achieved all our strategic goals, what would we look like five or ten years from now?

In contrast, a *mission statement* is a concise explanation of the organization's reason for existence—its *raison d'être*. It describes the company's purpose and overall intention. The mission statement supports the vision and communicates purpose and direction to employees, customers, vendors, and other stakeholders. The mission statement reveals answers to these questions:

- What is our organization's purpose?
- Why does our organization exist?

In other words, a vision statement focuses on the *future*, while a mission statement focuses on the *present*.

The most impactful mission and vision statements are brief and easy to understand and remember.

Example: Here are examples of two well-known companies' mission and vision statements:

	Mission Statement	Vision Statement
Amazon	We strive to offer our customers the lowest possible prices, the best available selection, and the utmost convenience.	To be Earth's most customer-centric company, where customers can find and discover anything they might want to buy online.
Tesla	To accelerate the world's transition to sustainable energy.	To create the most compelling car company of the 21st century by driving the world's transition to electric vehicles.

Why a Company's Vision and Mission Matter

Why are vision and mission statements important?

First, because even though companies *exist* to generate revenue or add to shareholder value, they will *thrive* by providing a deeper, more compelling solution to people's needs. Employees who are passionate about the company's mission often fall in love with their work, experience higher productivity levels and engagement, and express loyalty to the company. This can lead to longer tenures that ultimately can benefit the organization's bottom line over time.

Second, companies that stand for something meaningful are much more likely to attract top talent.

Key Points

1. There is a difference between a vision statement and a mission statement. A company's *vision statement* looks forward and creates a mental image of the ideal state that the organization's leadership wishes to achieve. It is inspirational and aspirational and should challenge employees. In contrast, a mission statement is a concise explanation

of the organization's reason for existence. It describes the company's purpose. The *mission statement* supports the vision and communicates purpose and direction to employees, customers, vendors, and other stakeholders. In other words, a vision statement focuses on the future, while a mission statement focuses on the present.

2. By performing the simple act of memorizing the corporate mission and vision statements, and then demonstrating your awareness of them, you will certainly increase your visibility within the organization. You also will distinguish yourself as someone who has the potential to take on more responsibilities and rise through the ranks of the company.

3. It is critically important for a company's actions to be consistent with its mission.

Action Steps

1. When you are interviewing with companies, read, understand, and prepare well for your interviews. During the interview process, mention and ask questions about the company's mission and vision.

2. As a result of your inquiries, if you find that your own passions are well-aligned with the company's mission, let it be known. Demonstrating a passion for a company's mission is a compelling reason for them to make you an offer and for you to accept it. Plus, you will have already enhanced your future career path.

3. Memorize your company's mission statement, and be passionate about your role in pursuing it. Write your company's mission statement below, and study it often so you can align your career trajectory with it:

_____

_____

_____

_____

4. Memorize your company's vision statement so you can align your decisions with it. Write your company's vision statement below:

_____

_____

_____

_____

_____

5. Take opportunities to convey your understanding and buy-in of your company's mission and vision statements. You might appear arrogant if you display your ability to recite the mission or vision statements. Don't recite them; instead, you can simply and tactfully convey your knowledge by communicating in statements like the following: "This initiative by the company makes so much sense in light of our mission to _____" or "This project is a brilliant way to accelerate our path to achieving our vision of _____."

Caution

As a relatively new employee, if you observe actions that seem inconsistent with your company's corporate mission, do not overreact. Bring it up in a non-confrontational, non-threatening way with your immediate supervisor. Early in your career, you don't want to appear to be challenging the wisdom of decisions made by superiors.

Prayer

Pray for the Holy Spirit to help you understand your company's mission and vision and to align your career path with those important guidelines. Ask the Lord to help you recognize and pursue opportunities to contribute to the company's mission and vision:

Gracious and Loving God:

Thank you for giving me the opportunity to work at this company. You have great plans for me, plans to give me hope and a future (Jere. 29:11). I ask for your help to see how the skills and personality you imbued in me fit with the vision and mission of this organization. Guide me and show me ways to do my part in contributing to a realization of the company's goals for your glory. In the name of Jesus, amen.

Chapter 8

DEVELOP CULTURAL AND ORGANIZATIONAL AWARENESS

"Let the wise listen and add to their learning, and let the discerning get guidance."

Proverbs 1:5

In any environment, it pays to be keenly aware of what's going on around you. This is certainly the case when you are navigating a new work environment. The more you observe how people interact with one another and how important projects and tasks get done, the better you will be able to shine in your professional role. However, even before accepting a new position, it is important to identify any inappropriate elements of the company's culture that may conflict with your own value system.

What Is Culture?

Culture is an organization's identity. It's a somewhat elusive concept because you can't measure it. In essence, it's the "vibe" of an organization. It's the atmosphere, the environment, the "feel" of a company.

Sometimes people think a company's culture is all about the perks it offers, but a culture is much more than that. Culture encompasses the values, mission, and vision of a company's leaders.

Natalie Baumgartner, PhD, is the Chief Workforce Scientist for an employee-engagement platform called Achievers. She says it's important for a company's culture to be defined in a very simple and accessible way so everyone from the CEO all the way down to the junior-most employee can understand it. Baumgartner writes, "Culture is really the small set of values that determine how you do things in your organization on a daily basis. These values should drive the three main buckets of business behavior: how you communicate, what you prioritize, and what gets rewarded."[6]

Why It's Important to Understand a Company's Culture

Every company has a unique culture. The more aware you are of the culture in your organization, the more easily you will be able to understand it, navigate it, and contribute to it. It takes some level of immersion into the organization and curiosity to acquire this knowledge.

One way to discover your company's culture and how things get accomplished is by networking throughout the company, with people at all different levels of the corporate hierarchy. The knowledge you gain about your organization and its culture will greatly facilitate your transition to increased responsibility.

Contribute Value throughout the Company

As you interface with those in your network, remember the advice given in chapter 7 to consider ways in which you can offer your assistance to others outside your own departmental contacts.

For several years as president of New York Life, I arranged monthly breakfast meetings with six or seven employees from different departments, most of whom didn't know each other. At those meetings, I talked about the company's recent successes and strategies and then asked each person to introduce himself or herself and elaborate on the following topics:

A. Their role within the organization
B. How they personally contribute to the mission of the organization

It was an engaging activity, and the feedback I received from those sessions was remarkably strong. Most attendees indicated that they had learned a lot they hadn't known about the company and about their colleagues. In many cases, long-term, highly productive cross-departmental relationships developed.

Key Points

1. Culture is an organization's identity. Culture encompasses the values, mission, and vision of a company's leaders.

2. Culture is really the small set of values that determine how you do things in your organization on a daily basis. These values should drive how you communicate, what you prioritize, and what gets rewarded.

3. As you learn more about your company's culture and how things get accomplished, ideation (a process for bringing forth innovative or creative new ideas) can be a great way for you to gain recognition and visibility within your department and beyond.

4. Learning the nature of your company's culture can be an important prerequisite for understanding the company's strategies and for developing your own strategic thinking capability, which are discussed in chapter 9.

Action Steps

1. As suggested, make sure you promptly distinguish yourself from your colleagues by memorizing your company's mission and vision statements. Don't recite them to anyone, but mention them when discussing how various projects and initiatives might contribute to those important statements. Few people take the time to do this, and once you do it, you will deliver instant value in the eyes of your leaders and peers.

2. To discover your company's culture and how things get accomplished, network throughout the company with people at all different levels of the corporate hierarchy.

3. As you build your network, ask your colleagues in your own department and those in other departments the following questions. Questions like these are excellent conversation-starters and will also demonstrate your interest in your coworkers.

- What is your role and your place within the organizational structure?
- How do you contribute to the organization's mission?
- What are some of your recent successes?
- What are some frustrations you have experienced?
- What projects have you worked on (or are now working on) that have required interfacing with other departments?
- If multiple departments take part in major projects, how is that effort coordinated, who has authority to make decisions, and are there any matrix-reporting relationships (i.e., situations in which an employee has a split reporting relationship to more than one boss).
- Does our company have a formal process for bringing forth innovative or creative new ideas? (This is sometimes referred to as *ideation*.)
- What are your candid views about how the process is working, and in what ways do you believe the process could be improved?

After your conversations with your coworkers (not during them), jot down some key points that you learned while speaking with each coworker.

Caution

Even before you accept a new position, learn what you can about a company's culture by doing your own pre-interview research. Then during interviews, ask the interviewers how they would describe the corporate culture. As a Christian, you must anchor yourself in following Christ. Any element of a corporate culture that seems at odds with your beliefs should be an indication that the company is not acting in concert with your own values. Factor this heavily into your decision to accept or decline the job offer.

Prayer

Call on the Holy Spirit to help you develop cultural and organizational awareness. Pray for guidance in navigating any aspects of your company's culture that do not align with your personal values and goals:

Gracious and Loving God:

You are loving and kind. It says in your Word that you are love and that you desire us to love you and each other (John 13:34–35)—fellowship is important to you. Please be with me as I meet and interact with others at this company. Help me grow my understanding of the culture and learn how to engage with it while keeping to the values you've outlined in Scripture. Help me see how this organization operates, day in and day out, so I can better contribute to its success. In the name of Jesus, amen.

Chapter 9

DEVELOP AND DEMONSTRATE
STRATEGIC THINKING CAPABILITY

"Do you not know that in a race all the runners run, but only one gets the prize? Run in such a way as to get the prize."
1 Corinthians 9:24

According to the *Business Dictionary*, *strategic thinking* is "the ability to come up with effective plans in line with an organization's objectives within a particular economic situation. Strategic thinking helps business managers review policy issues, perform long-term planning, set goals, determine priorities, and identify potential risks and opportunities."

If you can develop and demonstrate strategic thinking capability, you will stand out—not only among new and young employees, but even among more seasoned and long-tenured employees. In my corporate experience, even many senior officers of large companies simply didn't understand the difference between *strategy* and *tactics*.

Some people believe strategic thinking is an inherent talent that individuals either possess or don't. They think there is little way to develop such capability if you don't already possess the "gift." Even though (in chapter 1) I identified strategic leadership as one of my spiritual gifts, I believe that anyone can develop a strategic-thinking capability using the advice provided in this chapter, In fact, my own strategic capabilities were enhanced greatly through the effective mentoring of my own superiors, who were highly strategic in their thoughts and actions.

The Difference between Strategy and Tactics

Many employees—and some managers and leaders—don't understand the difference between *strategy* and *tactics*.

Strategy is how to leverage a company's core competencies to achieve its objectives and create sustainable competitive advantage. *Tactics* describe the specific actions that will be taken along the way.

Many people incorrectly think the difference between strategy and tactics is that strategy is long-term, and tactics are short-term. But both strategy and tactics can be either short-term or long-term.

Strategy is our path or bridge for going from where we are today to our goal. It's our general resource allocation plan. For example, one strategy might be to engage industry thought leaders to become advocates for our product. The related *tactics* are how we will specifically or tangibly do that. They might include direct-marketing letters, face-to-face meetings, key talking point scripts, and an iPad app. In general, if you can reach out and physically touch it, it's a tactic.[7]

Key Points

1. There is a difference between strategy and tactics. The word "strategy" was originally used as a war term in determining the means by which a combatant would defeat the enemy. In general, strategy in business is about beating the competition. Strategy is how to leverage a company's core competencies to achieve its objectives and create sustainable competitive advantage. In contrast, tactics describe the specific actions that will be taken along the way.

2. The first step in your learning process is to understand your own company's strategies.

Action Steps

1. Learn your company's strategies by taking the following actions:
   - Read your company's annual report, and ask for copies of the most recent strategic plan.
   - If your company has publicly traded stock, read the periodic reports of the analysts who follow that stock. There you can learn a lot more about the external view of your company's risks and opportunities and how it fares against the competition.
   - View reports of the various rating agencies, such as Moody's, S&P, and Fitch, which might be rating your company for creditworthiness or other purposes.
   - Search for recent articles and press releases.

2. Learn about your company's competition. Follow the same steps you used to research your own company, and research five or more key competitors. This task might be more difficult than researching your own company, but it will be well worth your time and effort. As you learn more about each competitor, keep notes on what you find out about each one because over time, their strategic efforts and positioning may change. Here are some tips for gathering information on competitors:
   - Read as much publicly available material as you can.
   - Mystery-shop the competition. If you really want to take your due diligence up a notch, and your business is in retail product sales, purchase some of the competitor's products to compare them against comparable products sold by your company.
   - Set up a Google alert for your own company and for its competitors. You will discover what's being said and reported about all the companies. You can find instructions for setting up a Google alert at https://support.google.com/websearch/answer/4815696?hl=en.
   - Get acquainted with distributors. They are out in the field, talking with your company's customers. They are likely to hear

opinions about your competitors' products and services—specifically about features your competitors offer that your company does not. Ask if there are some aspects of your business offerings that they would like to see expanded or modified.

- Review competing companies' websites.

3. Convert the knowledge you've learned about your company's strategies, and those of your competitors, into strategic thinking by thoughtfully considering the following questions. The answers to these questions will help you demonstrate a strong strategic thinking capability. As you learn more about the company and its competitors, jot down answers to these questions:

- How does my company currently differentiate itself from its key competitors?

_____

_____

_____

- What do we do differently and/or better than anybody else? Can we build on that, and if so, how?

_____

_____

_____

- What unique products, product features, or benefits does my company have that others don't have? Are there others we should be considering?

_____

_____

_____

- Are there consumer needs or desires that my company and/or its competitors are not currently meeting? What are ways we can meet those needs?

  _____

  _____

  _____

- How does my company compare to its competitors in customer surveys and reviews relating to products or services? If we fall short in some areas, what types of cost-effective investments can we make to significantly improve in those areas?

  _____

  _____

  _____

- How does our advertising, marketing, and branding stack up against the competition? How can we improve in this regard?

  _____

  _____

  _____

- Are there market segments that our competition is not adequately penetrating that we can effectively expand into?

  _____

  _____

  _____

- From a competitive employment perspective, how do our compensation and benefits compare to those of our key competitors? To what extent do we need to improve our own compensation and benefit packages to better compete for talent?

_____

_____

_____

If you have done your homework, asking yourself these questions and then answering them should trigger many strategic ideas that could help your company create sustainable competitive advantage.

As you communicate your thoughts and ideas to your company's management team, they will begin to recognize you as a highly strategic thinker with high potential for more senior roles in the organization.

Caution

Again, before offering suggestions for improvement, ask the Holy Spirit for guidance. Rather than proactively raising all such issues immediately with management, rely on the Holy Spirit to create those opportunities for you—and also to nudge you if you are not recognizing them.

Prayer

Call on the Holy Spirit to guide you in developing strategic thinking ability. Pray that the Lord will help you examine each situation in your workplace, develop strategic solutions, and communicate them with discretion:

Gracious and Loving God:

Dear Lord, you are wise in all your ways. I ask, like Solomon did, for wisdom (James 1:5). I especially ask for wisdom to navigate the workplace opportunities and situations you put before me. Help me understand and embrace the documented company strategies and to discern the unspoken strategic wisdom that you would share with this company through me. I ask for your help to communicate these ideas with the right heart, void of pride or presumption, in your perfect timing that your will would unfold. In the name of Jesus, amen.

Chapter 10

UNDERSTAND THE FINANCIAL
UNDERPINNINGS OF THE BUSINESS

"Listen to advice and accept discipline, and at the end you will be counted among the wise."
                              Proverbs 19:20

"I will instruct you and teach you in the way you should go; I will counsel you with my loving eye on you."
                              Psalm 32:8

As the president of New York Life Insurance Company, I saw many young people, and even high-level executives, place self-imposed limits on their advancement because they paid little or no attention to their companies' financial results. Nor did they appropriately consider the financial impact of their decisions.

The Biggest Career Blocker

Later, as I thought about my New York Life experience, I asked myself, "What is the biggest career blocker and deficiency among employees at all levels?"

The answer came to me quickly: they simply don't understand or appreciate the importance of financial results. Too often, people focus solely on top-line sales and revenue growth, almost to the exclusion of balancing a budget and achieving a strong bottom line or profit. Even worse, too many executives can't even read a financial statement, much less manage to one.

Focus on Top-Line and Bottom-Line Growth Simultaneously

The term *top-line* typically refers to a company's revenues, which are largely generated by sales of the company's products and services for the accounting period. The term *bottom line* refers to the company's net profits for the same accounting period.

In my experience as a president of a Fortune 100 company and as a director of several for-profit corporations, I have observed that most executives aspire to run a business. They often say, "I want to manage a P&L" (a profit-and-loss statement)." They even vigorously campaign for such opportunities within their organizations.

The primary reason many never get the opportunity (or worse, fail when they do get the opportunity) is that they don't recognize this simple fact: the key to success in business and in career advancement is not in achieving strong top-line growth or strong bottom-line growth, but rather in *accomplishing both simultaneously*. This is equally true whether you are working for a large public corporation, for a small business, or in a burgeoning entrepreneurial venture.

In many businesses, it's easy to achieve impressive top-line growth if you're not concerned with the bottom line—just undercut the competition in pricing and overpay distributors. Doing so can produce dramatic sales growth, but at the expense of the bottom line. That's not a sustainable proposition.

Conversely, it is relatively easy in the short run to achieve strong bottom-line growth if you're not concerned about top-line growth—just cut costs significantly while underpaying and overworking your employees and ignoring the quality of customer service. Such a strategy almost always leads to business failures, despite short-term bottom-line profits.

I have encountered top executives making seven-figure incomes who couldn't successfully run a business. Why? Because they focused almost exclusively on top-line revenue growth but either ignored, or didn't understand, the bottom-line profit impacts of their decisions.

As your knowledge increases about your company's financial underpinnings, I wouldn't be surprised if the CEO of your company, even if it's a large one, will hear that you are asking questions to learn more about this topic. Many young people have told me that it happened to them when they followed this simple advice.

Key Points

1. Even if financial acumen is not one of your spiritual gifts as identified in the exercise in chapter 1 of this book, you can still get labeled as a high-potential employee by taking some simple steps.
2. It's sufficient for you to know how the income statement is constructed and how it flows into the balance sheet during each accounting period. You don't need to know the details of how every accounting entry is determined.
3. Focus on top-line and bottom-line growth simultaneously. The key to success in business and in career advancement is not in achieving strong top-line growth or strong bottom-line growth, but rather in accomplishing both simultaneously.
4. The killer question for any business is "What drives the profitability of our business?"

Action Steps

For each of the action steps below, track your progress over time using the space provided.

1. To gain at least a basic knowledge of the key elements of your company's balance sheet and income statement, seek out someone

from the Finance or Accounting Department who is willing to spend a little time with you to provide a high-level understanding of financial reports.

_____

_____

_____

_____

_____

2. Once you have developed a rudimentary knowledge of your company's balance sheet and income statement, take the following actions to help distinguish yourself from most other employees—and even from many senior officers in the company:

A. Develop a spreadsheet that tracks (on a quarterly basis) the three highest-level summary numbers from the income statement (Revenues, Expenses, and Net Profit/Loss) and three from the balance sheet (Assets, Liabilities, and Net Equity). Then watch the changes from quarter to quarter. Taking a few minutes to update that sheet every quarter might be the best investment of time you'll ever make in your career.

_____

_____

_____

_____

_____

B. Once you gain comfort and confidence with the quarterly results, expand your understanding by going back to the person in Accounting to ask the killer question: "What drives the profitability of our business?"

_____

_____

_____

_____

C. Later, expand your knowledge into a more granular understanding by asking for breakouts of the key drivers, by business unit.

_____

_____

_____

_____

3. As you advance in your career, keep in mind that most decisions you make should be informed by their financial implications. Go back often to the important drivers identified in the answers to *the killer question.*

_____

_____

_____

_____

Caution

Combine the advice in this chapter and the other more practical chapters with the advice in chapters 1 through 5 on biblical principles in the workplace. In addition to being informed by financial implications, your decisions must be consistent with your values and beliefs, they must be aligned with the Golden Rule, and they must be decisions and actions your workplace partner—Jesus—would find pleasing.

Prayer

Ask the Lord to open your mind to a better understanding of your company's financial results. Then listen for His instruction and advice, as communicated to you through the Holy Spirit and facilitated by knowledgeable colleagues at the company. Pray for guidance in understanding the concepts well enough to apply the knowledge to your specific role. Pray that, if you do not consider yourself to be gifted in this area, the Lord will ease your anxiety and make you open to learning enough about this topic to benefit your organization and your own career:

Gracious and Loving God:

Lord, I ask for your favor and opportunities to learn more about my company's financial results (Ps. 90:17). This may not be my greatest strength, but I ask for your divine grace to open my mind to financial concepts in ways that will allow me to give my best to this organization in the role I have, glorifying you. In the name of Jesus, amen.

Chapter 11

TAKE CHARGE OF YOUR OWN DEVELOPMENT

"Lazy hands make for poverty, but diligent hands bring wealth."
Proverbs 10:4

In a sense, this entire book is about self-development. Some aspects of self-development are covered in other chapters—for example, abiding by The Golden Rule in chapter 5; preparing for meetings in chapter 12; strengthening your presentation skills in chapter 13; and balancing faith, family, and career in chapter 15.

Your Management Team Might Not Focus on Your Personal Development

No matter what your position is within your company, don't assume that your superiors will closely monitor, take a strong interest in, or offer to contribute to your development. You might need to take charge of your own professional development, even if it means using some of your evenings, weekends, or vacation time to participate in developmental activities.

Of all the chapters in this workbook, the advice in this one can and should be staged over time. Much of it will be most relevant after you have been on the job for a couple of years or longer. Over time, you can come back to the recommendations in this workbook periodically to review the recommendations for ongoing developmental advice.

There is no cookie-cutter approach to development; it needs to be customized for your own work situation and specific needs.

My Own Development Experience

I started my insurance career as an actuarial student at John Hancock Mutual Life Insurance Company in Boston. As an actuarial student, I was expected to achieve professional designations, which required passing an extremely difficult series of nine professional examinations. Even though I was paid a salary, my primary day-to-day responsibility was to study for those exams while taking on occasional projects. For almost three years, I didn't even know who my boss was, and I was rarely given any meaningful assignments. For some extended periods, I had no work assignments at all.

I was forced to find my own work and to take steps to develop myself. As it turns out, that was one of the best things that ever happened to me. It got me started down a path of self-development that led to much more gratification and success than if I had simply sat back and tried to enjoy being paid to do almost nothing, other than study for the exams.

Key Points

1. Recent trends suggest that pressure on corporate profits has led to sometimes extreme expense controls. This not only stresses out the workforce; it also results in companies limiting their expenditures on training and development.

2. Decades of research now point to emotional intelligence as being the critical factor that sets star performers apart from the rest of the pack. The connection is so strong that 90 percent of top performers have high emotional intelligence.[8]

Action Steps

1. Build your professional-development plan by taking the following important steps:

A. Create a vision of where you want to be in five years. Describe here what your ideal work situation will be in five years. What will your career look like? What role will you be in at that point?

_____

_____

_____

_____

_____

_____

B. Describe how your professional goals align with your company's mission and vision:

_____

_____

_____

_____

_____

C. Develop a plan to achieve the necessary skills to reach that goal; indicate an expected timetable for these pursuits. Write below the skills you will need to master to reach those goals, how you plan to achieve those goals, and the expected time frame in which you will complete them:

The Skill I Will Need	How I Will Achieve It	When I Will Complete It
Example: *Improve my presentation skills.*	*Join Toastmasters, and achieve my Competent Toastmaster (CTM) certificate.*	*One year from the end of next month*

D. Track your progress against the plan.

E. Review the plan regularly, and revise it as needed because your work situation will most likely change over time.

2. Approach your personal development in four broad categories. Identify those that will aid you the most in achieving your vision. Build your plan with a timetable around those areas of greatest and most urgent need. Here are the four categories, along with strategies you can take in each category to grow professionally:

   A. Adjust your mind-set.
      • Develop a growth mentality.
      • Define your success based on your beliefs and values.
      • Be willing to take on new changes.
      • Take initiative on your own behalf.

   B. Increase your productivity.
      • Improve your time management.
      • Prioritize.
      • Maintain a "to-do" list.

   C. Remain current in your field of expertise.
      • Seek out educational experiences.

- Bring back actionable ideas from your training.
- Participate in professional organizations.

D. Hone your people skills.

- Expand your internal network.
- Get to know your colleagues.
- Listen intently.
- Develop emotional intelligence—control your emotions and increase your level of empathy.

Describe what you will do in the next year to accomplish goals in these four categories, and specify your time frame:

Category of Personal Development	How I Will Improve in This Area	When I Will Complete This Step
1. Adjust my mind-set	**Example:** *Ask my manager for feedback so I can accelerate my professional growth.* **My strategy:**	**Example:** *In our next one-on-one meeting* **My time frame:**

Category of Personal Development	How I Will Improve in This Area	When I Will Complete This Step
2. Increase my productivity	**Example:** *Prioritize my assignments, and delegate the tasks I can.* **My strategy:**	**Example:** *Ongoing, but begin by the end of this month* **My time frame:**
3. Remain current in my field of expertise	**Example:** *Join the* _____ *organization and contribute actively.* **My strategy:**	**Example:** *By the end of next month* **My time frame:**

Category of Personal Development	How I Will Improve in This Area	When I Will Complete This Step
4. Hone my people skills	**Example:** *Meet at least two new people throughout the company each month, and find out how I can help them accomplish their goals. Keep a log.* **My strategy:**	**Example:** *Start next week.* **My time frame:**

3. Develop a growth mentality. Recognize that you will either stagnate at your current level or you will accept the challenge and effort required to grow and develop. Commit to doing what it takes to enable your own professional growth:

   A. Project out five years to identify what you believe will define success for you professionally at that point. To be successful in five years, what do you need to accomplish?

   _____

   _____

   _____

   _____

B. Be willing to take on new challenges and step out of your comfort zone. List three new challenges you will take that seem a bit uncomfortable now but will help you grow professionally:

_____

_____

_____

4. Improve your time management. According to a web survey by America Online and Salary.com, the average worker admits to frittering away 2.09 hours per day, not counting lunch. Supervisors notice who is making good use of their time and who is not. List three ways you can make better use of your time (for example, checking email fewer times a day, listing your priorities each day when you leave work so you can "hit the ground running" the next morning, or reorganizing the folders and files on your computer):

_____

_____

_____

Cautions

1. The list of action steps for this chapter is long and includes many things I did during my career—but certainly not within the first year or two of employment. If you attempt to do so too quickly, you will risk rapidly burning out or worse, sacrificing the attentiveness you need to give to your primary job responsibilities. Based on your most immediate needs, prioritize and stage these efforts.

2. Give priority attention to your own job responsibilities, learn about other areas within the organization as time permits.

3. No matter what your position is within your company, don't assume that your superiors will closely monitor and take a strong interest in your development. You must take charge of it yourself, even if it means using some of your evenings, weekends, or even vacation time to attend developmental activities.

Prayer

Call on the Holy Spirit to help you commit to a lifetime of learning. Pray that the Lord will lead you to, and help you recognize, opportunities to grow professionally. Ask Him to create in you a hunger for further knowledge and to use that new knowledge to benefit the organization you work for:

Gracious and Loving God:

It says in Proverbs 2:6 that you give wisdom and that from your mouth come knowledge and understanding. I ask that you would impart a measure of this to me, creating a development plan for my professional growth. Help me to be sensitive to the needs of those around me and the needs of this organization. Show me ways to improve my skills and emotional intelligence so I can be the best I can be, representing you well at this company. In the name of Jesus, amen.

Chapter 12

OVERPREPARE FOR EVERY MEETING

"And let us consider how we may spur one another on toward love and good deeds, not giving up meeting together, as some are in the habit of doing, but encouraging one another—and all the more as you see the Day approaching."
Hebrews 10:24–25

New employees are often invited to attend meetings and, at times, are asked to perform menial tasks like taking notes. Regardless of why you are in attendance and what you are expected to do (even if the expectation is to sit quietly and listen), take the time to overprepare.

I encourage you to prepare for every meeting early so you have adequate time to be ready to participate. This will reduce any anxiety you might be feeling about the meeting.

Many Employees Are Afraid to Speak Up at Work

As a new employee, you might feel hesitant about speaking up during a meeting. That might be the right instinct, but depending on the culture in your company, your comments might be welcome. Follow the tips in this chapter to prepare for meetings and to feel far more comfortable in participating in the discussions.

Being afraid to speak up is a common issue, even among employees who have been in their positions for a while. But staying silent about important issues can be costly to companies.

I recommend that you speak up when you feel your comments are contributing value to the discussion in a meeting. If you are unsure about the extent to which you are welcome to comment, speak about it with your manager or with the meeting's organizer before attending.

Poorly Organized Meetings Waste Time and Money

New and veteran employees alike often feel frustrated about having to participate in meetings that seem pointless.

As your tenure increases at your company, you can make a valuable contribution toward helping your peers conduct meetings that are more efficient, organized, and useful. However, the advice in this chapter is more about attending meetings than it is about organizing or running meetings.

If you are new to your company or to the workforce, you probably won't be asked to chair a meeting until you have gained some experience. However, if your job does require you to conduct meetings, plenty of resources are available online that can help you gain insights on organizing and chairing a meeting.

Key Points

1. A 2018 report by leadership training company VitalSmarts revealed that employees who keep silent about a problem, process, or strategy that just isn't working out—often because they're worried about being labeled as complainers or fear retaliation—can cost companies in productivity. But speaking up can help you fast-start your career, when it's appropriate to do so.[9]

2. Because many people consider meetings to be a waste of time, they often show up unprepared and/or with a negative mind-set. By viewing every meeting as an opportunity to gain knowledge, and by

overpreparing, you will distinguish yourself as a valuable employee with leadership potential.

Action Steps

1. If you are invited to a meeting, you are likely to receive some form of communication inviting you to attend. The invitation will probably include the information listed below, an agenda and possibly some advance reading materials to review. Before the meeting, make sure you understand these materials; ask the meeting organizer questions, if necessary:

    A. The date, time, and location of the meeting

    B. The purpose or objectives of the meeting

    C. The topics to be covered and who will cover each of them

    D. A list of other invitees

    E. Attachments containing materials to be read in advance of the meeting

2. It's important to read the attachments well before the meeting so you have adequate time to follow up on things you may not fully understand in preparation for the meeting.

3. In addition to making sure your calendar is clear for the meeting date and time, consider what is on your calendar immediately before the meeting time to be certain that you won't risk being late for the meeting, You might also need a one- or two-hour buffer before the meeting to gather your thoughts and refresh yourself on any previously distributed materials.

4. Find out before the meeting what the purpose is and what the intended outcomes will be. If that is not clear in the invitation, then don't hesitate to call the organizer of the meeting to find out.

5. Look at the topics to be discussed at the meeting and who the presenters will be. If there is no material provided for advance reading, or if you feel you aren't knowledgeable about the topic, consider asking for reading material. If it still is not clear to you,

set up a meeting with one or more of the presenters to ask a few questions before the meeting.

6. Even if you will be an inactive participant in the meeting, identify questions that might be directed to you during the meeting, and be ready with answers.

7. Take notes in the meeting. Write down things that you don't totally understand and will need to follow up on.

8. If you will be an active participant, speak to the organizer of the meeting to understand your role. Write out questions and comments for all topics.

Cautions

1. Early in your career, attendance at meetings is a learning experience, as opposed to an opportunity to display your knowledge. Don't risk appearing arrogant by leaping into the conversation inappropriately—perceived arrogance is a major career blocker.

2. If your colleagues complain about meetings they view as a waste of time, resist the temptation to join them. Maintain your positive attitude, and try to point out positive outcomes of those meetings. Or suggest ways to make them more valuable and enjoyable.

Prayer

Pray for the Holy Spirit to help you see the value in every meeting you attend and to contribute to each meeting in a way that glorifies the Savior and enhances your professional reputation. Pray that you never begin to grumble or complain about having to attend meetings:

Gracious and Loving God:

Help me use every opportunity you put before me to speak as you lead me, with truth, boldness, and love all for your glory while giving my best in all situations. I ask for a humble, teachable heart—a heart that is willing to do what you ask without grumbling (Phil 2:14) and to do as my superiors ask with a sincere heart (Eph. 6:5). In the name of Jesus, amen.

Chapter 13

MAKE EVERY PRESENTATION A COMMAND PERFORMANCE

"In the same way, let your light shine before others, so that they may see your good works and give glory to your Father who is in heaven."
Matthew 5:16 (ESV)

When you are fortunate enough to be asked to make a presentation of any kind, always do what you can to make it a command performance. Seize the opportunity to show off your talents (but not in an arrogant way).

Consider It a Privilege, Not a Chore, to Make a Presentation

Throughout my career, I encountered many people who treated their presentations as a necessary but unwelcome job responsibility. It was as if they considered their presentations to be annoyances that interfered with their "real" work. And like a trip to the dentist, they were glad when it was over, and the pain subsided.

I held the opposite view. I have always believed that presentations provide you with an opportunity to showcase your knowledge and expertise; to lead, guide, and inform others; and to contribute to an organization's success.

For that reason, I always put a lot of thought and effort into my presentations—whether they were short presentations to a small group of employees or more in-depth presentations to a much larger group. Larger groups were often employees of a large division or department, a large "town hall" type meeting, or a presentation addressed to thousands of the company's agents. As my career advanced, I also had numerous opportunities to speak at industry meetings and eventually was honored to deliver a few college commencement addresses.

I gave the same level of attention to my preparation for each presentation, no matter what the audience or venue. In this chapter, I provide you with some useful tips on your own preparation.

Employers Want to Hire People with Polished Speaking Skills

There is a positive correlation between success and speaking ability. Being able to deliver your comments and expertise verbally in front of a group in an effective, persuasive way is a skill that many employers are seeking.

In a 2018 survey conducted by the Association of American Colleges and Universities, executives and hiring managers said good verbal communication is the skill they want most from job candidates. This skill outranked others that get far more public attention, such as critical thinking, solving complex problems, working in teams, and writing well. More than 80 percent of the executives and hiring managers surveyed said good verbal skills were important, and fewer than half said recent college graduates excel in this area.[10]

This is an area in which you can easily position yourself for career success, simply by following the recommendations I've made in this chapter.

Key Points

1. Being a skilled presenter is an area in which new employees can easily position themselves for career success.

2. When you tell a story to make a point, it will be much more interesting than if you simply present facts and data. Plus, your audience is much more likely to remember your key point if you deliver it using a story. Stories enhance message retention.

3. To deliver presentations effectively for your peers of all ages, it's important to achieve a balance between casual language used in texting and social media and more formal, classic language. Some older people might consider text-speak to be inappropriate for business presentations, and some younger people might not resonate well with presentations they consider too formal and stodgy.

Action Steps

1. Before every presentation, call on God to guide you, through His Holy Spirit, in what to say and how to deliver the message. Rely on the Holy Spirit to calm your nerves and to give you the right things to say. After every presentation, thank God for His assistance.

2. If you say something during a presentation that is not clear and can possibly be misinterpreted, learn from those mistakes, and avoid repeating them. View those experiences not as the Holy Spirit failing you in the presentation, but rather as God enhancing your development and evolution as a better communicator.

3. Follow these recommendations to enhance the quality of your presentation:
   - Know the interest level of the audience you will be addressing, as well as their level of knowledge and competency in the subject matter.
   - Get familiar with the venue, and know in advance how much time has been allotted for your remarks.
   - Identify in advance the four or five key points you want your audience to remember. In an oral presentation, a list of dozens of ideas won't be memorable and will only frustrate members of the audience. Speak only on topics on which you are considered an expert. If you have any doubts about your command of a particular topic, then do research to better prepare yourself.
   - Start with humor. Getting a laugh from the audience up-front is a great way to calm your own nerves.

- Tell stories. They are memorable and interesting.

- To structure a presentation so it has maximum impact, deliver the key message three times. At the beginning, tell your audience what you plan to discuss. Then, in the body of your presentation, discuss the topic. At the end, close by recapping what you told the audience. In this way, they know what's coming, they hear it, and then they are reminded of your key points.

- Whether you use PowerPoint, Prezi, or another presentation program, make sure your presentation has a lot of visual appeal. Where appropriate, include interactive elements, such as links to YouTube or other videos, to hold the interest of your audience. On each slide, include an interesting heading/title and a few bullet points. Avoid filling the slides with text or a lot of numbers.

- Practice your presentation until you can deliver it comfortably without reading from your notes. Be enthusiastic. Showcase your knowledge. And keep your original objective in mind as you are speaking.

- Allow a few minutes for a Q&A session. Giving your audience a chance to ask questions, and then answering them concisely but thoroughly, will provide clarification about any details your audience didn't fully understand.

4. Follow these tips when preparing your presentation:
   A. Begin with an outline, and then write your speech.
   B. Read the written speech out loud, just as if you were delivering it live. Revise words and points of emphasis as needed. Repeat this step after making modifications, and time yourself.
   C. Transform the written speech into bullet points. Initially, these might be quite long. Boldface or underline the key words in each bullet point.
   D. Try to deliver the speech from the bullet points without reading. Do this two or three times.

E. Shorten the bullet points again, and practice the talk out loud two or three more times. Each time you rehearse a delivery, you will further shorten the written bullet points.

Cautions

1. As you advance in your career, avoid slipping into a mind-set of complacency. Continue to consider every presentation an opportunity to shine.
2. Never read a speech to an audience, unless for some reason you are forced to use a teleprompter.

Prayer

Call on the Holy Spirit to help you adopt the mind-set that every presentation should be a command performance. Pray for wisdom in delivering the best possible presentation that is tailored to your audience so it enhances your professional image among your coworkers:

Gracious and Loving God:

You are the great storyteller—wise and charismatic. Please grant me the ability to weave stories and help convey ideas through my words with a right heart and clarity of purpose. I ask for your knowledge and courage to stand in front of others to impart the wisdom you want me to share with them. Teach me and guide me in your knowledge and truth (Ps. 25:4–5) so I can present ideas in a clear and compelling way. In the name of Jesus, amen.

Chapter 14

DEMONSTRATE INTEGRITY
AND EARN TRUST

"The integrity of the upright guides them, but the crookedness of the treacherous destroys them."

Proverbs 11:3 (ESV)

Integrity and *trustworthiness* are qualities that are essential to future success in any career. Few people focus on how to convey those qualities. Rather, they often simply rely on the ability of superiors, peers, and subordinates to discern those characteristics in them.

I have successfully coached many people on how to demonstrate integrity and earn trust. In addition, I have coached and mentored several young people on how to avoid the death knell of arrogance. Dealing with these issues (which often are largely perceptual) is particularly gratifying and meaningful for those who profess their Christianity yet don't realize they are inadvertently projecting the wrong persona.

How to Display Integrity at Work

Even if you consider integrity to be one of your core values, your integrity won't be apparent to those around you unless you take actions that display your integrity. Here are some ways to do that.

1. **Be Honest**

   Of course this means avoiding lies, but it also means avoiding exaggeration or even putting an inappropriately positive spin on a negative result. I used an expression with my employees that encouraged and welcomed full disclosure of bad news as well as good. I let them know I valued their willingness to "tell me what I needed to know, not what I wanted to hear." I couldn't deal with a problem I didn't know existed.

2. **Keep Your Word and Your Commitments**

   You will develop a reputation of integrity if you are meticulous about delivering on your promises and fulfilling your commitments. If you say you are going to do something, do it. Make every effort to complete it within the committed time frame.

3. **Be Accountable and Take Responsibility**

   Inevitably, you will make mistakes at work. The best way to display integrity is to admit to a mistake. Apologize if it has hurt someone else or damaged a relationship. Your reputation will flourish if you make a practice of "giving credit and taking blame."

How to Earn Others' Trust

Follow these tips to build trust with your peers, subordinates, and superiors.

1. **Praise the Work Others Do**

   Be quick to praise others in the workplace and give them credit for their work. In so doing, you will build trust and be perceived as a gracious person. While it may seem difficult to do this for someone whom you may perceive as a competitor, it will go a long way toward establishing a strong working relationship.

2. **Avoid Complaining or Gossiping**

   There is no quicker way to be distrusted than to be a complainer or a gossiper. Gossip is potentially lethal to a good relationship. Even if you are complaining or gossiping about others and the subject of your gossip or complaint never finds out about it (which is unlikely), the people you are complaining to will almost certainly wonder if you are also complaining or gossiping about them to others.

3. **Show Trust in Others**

This seems pretty obvious, but it really is true that if you demonstrate trust in others, they are likely to reciprocate. Until they prove otherwise, trust your coworkers to execute tasks they say they will do, to meet committed deadlines, and to be honest.

4. **Avoid Displaying Negative Body Language**

Use body language as a trust builder and sustainer, as opposed to a trust destroyer. It can be difficult to control your body language, but making a concerted effort to do so will go a long way to establishing trusting relationships.

Our faces and our posture often convey negative messages to someone who is speaking to us. Frowns, negative head nods, and even what we do with our eyebrows can communicate disagreement, skepticism, and anger. Sitting with your arms crossed on your chest or slouching in your chair can communicate an unwillingness to listen, disinterest, or disagreement.

Conversely, positive body language such as smiling, making eye contact, nodding your head affirmatively, and leaning into the conversation will make your coworkers comfortable. It will make them feel connected with you and will make them willing to engage more fully in providing their opinions and offering new ideas.

5. **Treat Your Coworkers with Respect and Dignity**

Remind yourself often that as a Christian, you recognize the worth of every human being. Someone's title or job grade doesn't change that fundamental belief. Reflect that in how you treat everyone, whether they are the CEO or someone from the custodial staff. Remember that in the eyes of the Lord, everyone else is just as important as you are.

If you fail to treat anyone in your organization with respect and dignity, it will be noticed, and you will risk conveying arrogance.

That can be a devastating roadblock to your future advancement. There's more on the topic of arrogance below.

6. **Be Humble and Occasionally Self-Deprecating**

Great leaders in any field, including business, often exhibit great humility, understate their accomplishments, and even joke about their shortcomings. Being self-deprecating shows people that you do not consider yourself to be superior to them.

Demonstrating integrity, being known as trustworthy, and being confident but not arrogant will make you far more likely to succeed and advance in an organization than employees who do not possess these qualities. Employers can teach technical skills, but they cannot teach valuable "soft" skills like integrity and trust. Demonstrating that you possess, and value, these characteristics will lay a solid foundation for your effectiveness and value to your organization.

Key Points

1. The great leaders of our time, whether in business or in any other profession, almost all seem to exhibit one consistent character trait: integrity.

2. Integrity and trustworthiness are qualities that are essential to future success in any career.

3. The perception that one is arrogant can be a barrier to success in the workplace. Dealing with such issues (which often are largely perceptual) is particularly gratifying and meaningful for those who profess their Christianity, yet don't realize they are inadvertently creating the wrong persona.

4. An employee who demonstrates integrity, is trustworthy, and is confident but not arrogant is far more likely to succeed and advance in an organization than an employee who does not possess those qualities.

Action Steps

1. To display integrity at work, always be honest. The saying "Honesty is the best policy" is as true in your work life as it is in your personal life.

2. Tell superiors and coworkers what they need to know, not what they want to hear. Those around you cannot deal with a problem if they don't know it exists.

3. You will develop a reputation of integrity if you are meticulous about delivering on your promises and fulfilling your commitments. If you say you are going to do something, do it.

4. When you make a mistake at work, admit it and apologize if it has hurt someone else or damaged a relationship. Your reputation will flourish if you make a practice of "giving credit and taking blame."

5. To earn others' trust at work, praise their work when it is warranted, avoid complaining or gossiping, show trust in others, avoid displaying negative body language, and treat your coworkers with respect and dignity.

6. Be humble and even occasionally self-deprecating—laugh at yourself.

7. Describe two situations that are examples of ways in which 1) you successfully achieved one of the directives above (in numbers 1 through. 6) and 2) an example of where you failed to do so:

    _____

    _____

    _____

8. Avoid any hint of arrogance. Once that perception exists, it is difficult to reverse it. Do a self-check for arrogance by assessing yourself in these areas. Rate yourself with lower scores, beginning with 1, if you feel you need work in an area. Rate yourself with higher scores if you feel you excel in this area:

Arrogance Self-Assessment

A. I recognize that I am human, and I make mistakes. I occasionally poke fun at myself.

   1   2   3   4   5   6   7   8   9   10

B. I regularly listen to and value other people's points of view. If they differ from mine, I try to learn from their perspectives.

   1   2   3   4   5   6   7   8   9   10

C. I am careful to avoid having an attitude of entitlement. I never demand, or suggest that I should receive, special treatment.

   1   2   3   4   5   6   7   8   9   10

D. I am always considerate of others. I avoid dominating every conversation and inappropriately interrupting others. I do not take advantage of my rank in a way that inconveniences others.

   1   2   3   4   5   6   7   8   9   10

E. I do not belittle others. I praise people in public and address my concerns with people in private.

   1   2   3   4   5   6   7   8   9   10

F. I am gracious. I go out of my way to praise the good work of others, no matter what their level in the organization. I notice their contributions and let them know I value what they do.

   1   2   3   4   5   6   7   8   9   10

Now, for those areas in which you gave yourself a score below 7, describe steps you can take to improve in those areas to avoid coming across as arrogant:

_____

_____

_____

_____

_____

Cautions

1. Avoid coming across as arrogant. In my view, arrogance is one of the greatest career blockers and one of the most difficult perceptions to overcome.

2. But don't confuse confidence with arrogance. There is nothing insulting about a healthy level of confidence.

3. I strongly caution you not to make the mistake of overcommitting to promises you might not be able to fulfill. If this happens, you will quickly develop the opposite reputation to the one you are trying to establish.

Prayer

Call on the Holy Spirit to guide you in demonstrating integrity and earning trust as you build your career and establish professional relationships:

Gracious and Loving God:

I ask for integrity and humility, praying 1 Peter 5:5 ESV for myself: "Likewise, you who are younger, be subject to the elders. Clothe yourselves, all of you, with humility toward one another, for 'God opposes the proud but gives grace to the humble.'" Help me love and respect those around me, bearing with others in love (Eph. 4:2) to lead by your example in truth and honesty. In the name of Jesus, amen.

Chapter 15

BALANCE FAITH, FAMILY, AND CAREER

"But as for me and my household, we will serve the LORD."
Joshua 24:15

Whether you are in the early stages of your career or you have advanced into greater responsibilities, the demands on your time can be quite extreme. With today's technology, we are hyperconnected to other people and to seemingly infinite amounts of data and information, available to us in a millisecond. But we all seem to be more overworked, less productive, and lonelier than ever.

The Dangerous Consequences of Overextending Yourself

Most companies have become more aggressive in pursuing higher profitability. One way to achieve that, in addition to greater revenue growth, is through cost reduction. As a result, despite significant improvements in technology in recent years, employees at all levels continue to be expected to produce more with fewer and fewer resources—including human resources. The output expected from an individual today is multiples of what was expected from an individual just a few years ago.

The unintended negative consequence and collateral damage from this environment is the negative impact on our personal and family lives.

According to numerous studies by Marianna Virtanen of the Finnish Institute of Occupational Health, overwork and the resulting stress can lead to all sorts of health problems, including the following:[11]

- Impaired sleep
- Depression
- Heavy drinking
- Diabetes
- Impaired memory
- Heart disease

The more hours we work, the less healthy we become. This is a costly outcome for our own health and our relationships as individuals. It's also detrimental to a company's bottom line because the consequences of overwork lead to increased absenteeism and turnover, decreased productivity, and rising employee dissatisfaction.

Productivity decreases when we scatter our attention. So how can we stay focused?

It all boils down to priorities. We are inundated with expectations, responsibilities, and self-exerted pressure to succeed to the point where we try to do everything well, all at once. It's just not possible. Quality is more important than quantity. We need to focus on what's truly important in our lives—often a balance of faith, family, and career—and a prioritization of those elements in our daily schedules.

We All Need Coping Skills

We all need to develop coping skills that enable us to balance the many priorities we are juggling.

Perhaps the most important coping technique that commenced for me and my family in 1984 was that I began taking each of my five children on annual trips alone with me for special one-on-one bonding experiences.

When the kids were young, even a trip up the road to a local hotel for two or three nights was an exciting adventure. As they became teenagers and young adults, we sought out more educational and cultural experiences. In each case, the important thing was not where we traveled, but rather the fact that we did it together. These trips became not only a family tradition but also a corporate legacy.

Even today, years after my retirement, the most frequent comment I receive in emails and holiday greeting cards from members of my extended family at New York Life is a "thank you" for sharing stories of those trips in presentations I made to employees and agents. Many of those employees and agents adopted a similar practice with their own families.

When we devote ourselves to our careers, it can be easy to get our lives out of balance and neglect our families and friends, our health, and our spirituality. Always be aware of the balance—or imbalance—in your life, and take steps to ensure that all aspects of your life are getting the attention from you that they need.

Key Points

1. I believe that to realize happiness and fulfillment in life, you must do the following:
   - Identify your spiritual gifts, and use them to serve the Lord.
   - Study the teachings of Jesus Christ, and live your life as He would have you live it.
   - Love God with all your heart, mind, and soul.
   - Love your neighbor as yourself.
   - Love yourself.

2. Today, it is impossible to complete every task and meet everyone's expectations. We must prioritize what's most important. The following have consistently been my top five priorities, ranked in order of their importance to me:
   - My relationship with Christ
   - My relationship with my wife, Sue
   - My relationship with my extended family

- My job
- My volunteer and leisure activities

Please note that just because you are committed to getting a fast start in your career, you do not have to list your job as your number-one priority. As you can see above, I listed my job as number four. I will readily admit that my priorities often slipped out of balance. Committing your priorities to writing and reviewing the list often will provide you with the impetus to rebalance when needed.

Action Steps

1. Define your highest priorities in life. Your job does not have to be number one! Always be aware of areas you are neglecting:

   A. _____

   B. _____

   C. _____

   D. _____

   E. _____

2. Develop coping techniques to help you reduce your stress level, enjoy life more, and balance your many priorities.

   Example: Seeing what other people have adopted as their coping mechanisms might help you discover your own. Here is a list of just a few of the personal coping techniques I've heard from others who have attended some of my speaking engagements and discussion forums:

   - Engaging in regular family prayer time and devotionals
   - Dedicating one-one-one chat time with each child and with their spouse
   - Attending special summer camps and events with family members
   - Expressing love daily—both verbal affirmations and hugs

- Coaching kids' sports teams

Now list some coping mechanisms that can help *you* relax and enjoy life more:

_____

_____

_____

_____

_____

Cautions

1. Avoid the temptation to try to excel in every area of your life all the time. We are all inundated with expectations, responsibilities, and self-exerted pressure to succeed to the point where we try to do everything well, all at once. It's just not possible. We must decide what's important and focus on that task. Recognize that quality is more important than quantity.

2. Always be aware of the need for balance in your life so you can try to avoid overextending yourself. Doing so can lead to serious health issues and personal problems.

Prayer

Pray that the Holy Spirit will give you awareness when your life is out of balance. Pray for discernment and wisdom in saying no to those activities that steer you away you're your biggest priorities in your life:

Gracious and Loving God:

You said your greatest two commandments are to love you with all my heart, all my soul, and all my mind and to love my neighbor as myself (Matt. 22:37–39). I ask for your help to prioritize the things in my life in accordance with these commands while being a positive representative of you in the workplace. Make a way for important matters in my life to align properly, with the time and energy to see them through as you desire. In the name of Jesus, amen.

ENJOY THE JOURNEY

As I have stated elsewhere in this workbook, my passion (both pre- and post-retirement) has been to positively impact the lives of others in service to the Lord. Some readers of the early manuscript of the book *Fast-Starting a Career of Consequence* suggested I split it into two books—one providing advice on following biblical principles in the workplace and the other on providing advice for fast-starting a career of consequence.

I strongly resisted those recommendations because I found the two topics not only to be a part of my DNA but inextricably linked in a symbiotic way that was a catalyst for rapid future personal growth, fulfillment, and happiness.

While I may have limited my audience of potential readers to some extent, I wanted to provide the most robust and meaningful advice I could give to those who chose to pick up the book or this workbook and read them. I could not decouple the importance of my faith from the valuable experiences of my business career.

Like most people, I learned from my mistakes and was energized by my successes. By following the advice in the book and the workbook, my hope and prayer is that you will avoid some of the mistakes I made and will enthusiastically embrace the action steps I am suggesting. This supplemental workbook will enable you to track your progress relative to the many action steps suggested.

There is a lot of guidance provided in these chapters. Please don't be overwhelmed or discouraged by the task at hand. Many dozens of people (Christians and non-Christians alike) have already benefited enormously simply by following the five original tips I gave to my daughter, Dena, that are detailed in chapters 6 through 10.

You, your family, and your company will all benefit even more if you adhere to the biblical principles of Chapters 1 through 5 and if you systematically exercise the recommended advice in all the other chapters, 6 through 15.

You don't need to implement all of the recommendations immediately, nor should you attempt to do so. As I point out in several chapters, the timing of many of the action steps I suggest should occur as you mature in your new role and as you develop relevant on-the-job experiences. You will benefit even more if you develop a plan to proceed at a deliberate but realistically timed pace while using your unique spiritual gifts and remaining true to your values and beliefs.

Now, after my long and successful career in business, God has helped me find ways in which I can effectively touch more lives and make better use of my own spiritual gifts. The exercise of writing the book and the workbook has enabled me to meaningfully serve the Lord in a new and exciting way. I hope and pray that as you read these resources, you will be inspired to embrace and implement the advice and, as a result, significantly enrich your future.

Congratulations on your entry or re-entry into the workplace! May the advice provided. in this workbook result in a richly fulfilling career of consequence. Enjoy the journey!

About the Author

After earning a bachelor's degree from Amherst College and a master's degree in statistics from Wayne State University, Frederick J. Sievert began his career as a junior high school mathematics teacher. He later entered the insurance business as an actuarial trainee. After a rapid rise to the top of the organization, with responsibility for 65,000 agents and employees worldwide, he ultimately retired in 2007 as president of the New York Life Insurance Company, a Fortune 100 corporation.

Following his early retirement at age fifty-nine, Sievert attended Yale Divinity School to enhance the spiritual development and education he felt he had neglected during his successful but intense career. He was awarded a master's degree in religion from Yale in 2011.

In retirement, Sievert is following his passion to serve the Lord by using his spiritual gifts to positively impact the lives of others in ways that reflect both his faith and his business experience.

In addition, he remains actively engaged in writing, teaching, mentoring young executives, serving on the boards of five nonprofit organizations and two for-profit corporations, and following his calling into the ministry created by his first book, *God Revealed: Revisit Your Past to Enrich Your Future*. His second book, *Grace Revealed: Finding God's Strength in Any Crisis*, recounts stories of people in severe crises who found relief and recovery through their faith and personal relationships with Christ.

Sievert has been in leadership roles in all the churches he has attended since he was in his twenties.

A frequent speaker, Sievert addresses audiences ranging in size from small book clubs and Bible-study classes to large national conventions. He has completed more than fifty TV and radio interviews, which include appearances on Fox & Friends, the Fox Business Channel, and the Daystar Christian network. Two of the stories from his second book were featured as videos on The 700 Club in May 2019.

Appendix

"SPIRITUAL GIFTS IN THE MARKETPLACE" ASSESSMENT

In this appendix is a highly useful spiritual assessment created by Darren Shearer, founder of the Theology of Business Institute.[12]

Darren says he created the *Spiritual Gifts in the Marketplace Assessment* because most of the other gift assessments seemed to be designed primarily to get people to volunteer at church on Sunday mornings. He created this tool specifically for Christian business professionals to help them understand that their spiritual gifts are applicable in the business world.

He has kindly provided permission for me to reprint his assessment here.

Instructions

1. For each of the spiritual gift recognition statements, please rate yourself on a scale of 1 to 10 in the corresponding blanks on the Response Sheet provided below (from page 87 of Darren's book): 1 = "Never," and 10 = "Always and without exception." You can download a blank copy of the Response Sheet at www.TheologyofBusiness.com/ResponseSheet.

2. For the most helpful results on this assessment:
   - Spend no more than 20 seconds on each item. Go with your first instinct. Your immediate response is best.

- Remember that the goal is not to score high for any of the spiritual gift recognition statements. The goal is to have variances among your responses so you can identify your primary spiritual gifts.
- Be as honest with your answers as possible. This will produce the most helpful results.

Spiritual Gift Recognition Statements

1. "I organize ideas, resources, time, and people effectively."
2. "Ministry leaders look to me for guidance."
3. "People tell me I am a compassionate person."
4. "I like introducing people to each other."
5. "I enjoy creating and/or inventing new things and new ways of doing things."
6. "I am passionate about connecting with people from other cultures and nationalities."
7. "I have a unique ability to sense whether or not a person is acting in accordance with God's will."
8. "Through inspirational words, I often have helped people to think more optimistically about themselves and the world around them."
9. "I have challenged other Christians to share their faith with non-Christians."
10. "I have found it somewhat easy to believe God for things that seemed impossible to others."
11. "I regularly give money beyond my tithe toward the Lord's work."
12. "People often tell me I made them feel welcome in a new place."
13. "I am passionate about praying to God on behalf of others."
14. "I spend a significant percentage of my time learning new things."
15. "People often tell me I am a gifted leader."
16. "I am passionate about pursuing opportunities to see God work miracles wherever I go."
17. "I often take the time to care for the emotional and/or spiritual needs of people around me."

18. "I have communicated to others timely and urgent messages that I believe came directly from God."
19. "People around me know they can count on me to help out."
20. "I am passionate about putting in the extra effort to explain complicated concepts in a simple way so that people can understand."
21. "I often speak to God in an unknown, heavenly language."
22. "I apply the truth of God's Word in my everyday life."
23. "Others have told me I helped to lead them into the presence of God."
24. "People have told me I am a good planner and organizer."
25. "I have started multiple new ministries."
26. "My heart hurts when I see others hurting."
27. "I have connected many like-minded people together."
28. "People have told me I am a very creative person."
29. "I gravitate toward people who are from different cultures and nationalities than mine."
30. "Others have told me I have a special ability to perceive things most people are not able to perceive."
31. "I am passionate about motivating people to be more courageous."
32. "I am passionate about sharing the Gospel message with all types of people."
33. "People tell me I have a large amount of faith."
34. "Giving is one of my favorite things to do."
35. "I have invited guests into my home on a regular basis."
36. "People ask me to pray for them because they know I will actually pray."
37. "My life demonstrates that I am passionate about learning new things."
38. "I prefer to focus on the bigger picture while other people work on the details."
39. "When people need a miracle to happen in their lives, such as a healing miracle, they often ask me to pray for them."

40. "I am passionate about connecting with, caring for, and coaching others one-on-one."
41. "I don't mind confronting people about their faulty thinking."
42. "I enjoy doing the tasks my leaders don't have time to do."
43. "I teach everywhere I go…not just in a classroom setting."
44. "To strengthen myself spiritually, I speak to my spirit regularly in an unknown, heavenly language."
45. "I intuitively find solutions to complicated problems."
46. "Throughout the day, I am keenly aware of the presence, majesty, and goodness of God."
47. "I enjoy figuring out what needs to get done to accomplish larger objectives."
48. "God tends to place me before influential people to represent Him and His Kingdom."
49. "I am passionate about helping to alleviate people's sufferings."
50. "People have told me I am good at networking."
51. "I have created many new things and/or new ways of doing things."
52. "People have told me I should be a missionary in another culture."
53. "I believe I have a special responsibility to sense when situations are spiritually unhealthy."
54. "People have told me they feel encouraged when they are around me."
55. "I have led many people to Jesus during my lifetime."
56. "I am passionate about trusting God to do big things."
57. "People who know me well would say I am a generous person."
58. "I am passionate about helping strangers to feel welcome when they are in my presence."
59. "I pray for extended amounts of time concerning the needs in our world."
60. "People view me as a source of information."
61. "I am passionate about getting other people involved and leveraging their unique abilities to accomplish large objectives."

62. "I have prayed for specific miracles, signs, wonders, and healings to happen and have seen many of them come to pass."
63. "People often share their personal struggles with me because they trust me."
64. "Other people have confirmed that they believe I speak God's truth about specific situations."
65. "I am eager to help even when others are not."
66. "People have told me I am a good teacher."
67. "I have spoken a message from God to others in an unknown, heavenly language that I or someone else interpreted."
68. "People often ask me how to deal with confusing situations."
69. "I set apart time every day to worship God and invite His presence into my life and into the atmosphere around me wherever I go."

You can download a blank PDF copy of this response sheet at www.TheologyofBusiness.com/ResponseSheet. It contains space to write your self-assessment for each of the sixty-nine questions, along with space to write your total point counts.

Response Sheet

Totals

1. ———	24. ———	47. ———	A. ———————
2. ———	25. ———	48. ———	B. ———————
3. ———	26. ———	49. ———	C. ———————
4. ———	27. ———	50. ———	D. ———————
5. ———	28. ———	51. ———	E. ———————
6. ———	29. ———	52. ———	F. ———————
7. ———	30. ———	53. ———	G. ———————
8. ———	31. ———	54. ———	H. ———————
9. ———	32. ———	55. ———	I. ———————
10. ——	33. ———	56. ———	J. ———————

11. ——	34. ——	57. ——	K. ————————
12. ——	35. ——	58. ——	L. ————————
13. ——	36. ——	59. ——	M. ————————
14. ——	37. ——	60. ——	N. ————————
15. ——	38. ——	61. ——	O. ————————
16. ——	39. ——	62. ——	P. ————————
17. ——	40. ——	63. ——	Q. ————————
18. ——	41. ——	64. ——	R. ————————
19. ——	42. ——	65. ——	S. ————————
20. ——	43. ——	66. ——	T. ————————
21. ——	44. ——	67. ——	U. ————————
22. ——	45. ——	68. ——	V. ————————
23. ——	46. ——	69. ——	W. ————————

Calculating the Results

For each line on the "Response Sheet," add the three numbers across for each letter, and write the totals next to each corresponding letter. (For example, your responses for #1 plus #24 plus #47 would add up to the amount you would place in the blank for "A," which is the gift of administration.) Then write in the corresponding spiritual gifts and circle your top three or four highest-scoring spiritual gifts.

A = Administration
B = Apostleship
C = Compassion
D = Connecting
E = Creativity
F = Cross-Cultural Ministry
G = Discernment
H = Encouragement
I = Evangelism

J = Faith

K = Giving

L = Hospitality

M = Intercessory Prayer

N = Knowledge

O = Leadership

P = Miracle-Working & Healing

Q = Pastoring

R = Prophecy

S = Service

T = Teaching

U = Tongues & Interpretation

V = Wisdom

W = Worship

Definitions and Examples

Refer to the following links for definitions of each spiritual gift, as well as an example of how each gift has been used in a business setting. The gifts correspond to lines A–W on the prior page.

(A) Administration:

www.TheologyofBusiness.com/GiftOfAdministration

(B) Apostleship:

www.TheologyofBusiness.com/GiftOfApostleship

(C) Compassion:

www.TheologyofBusiness.com/GiftOfCompassion

(D) Connecting:

www.TheologyofBusiness.com/GiftOfConnecting

(E) Creativity:

www.TheologyofBusiness.com/GiftOfCreativity

(F) Cross-Cultural Ministry:

www.TheologyofBusiness.com/GiftOfCrossCulturalMinistry

(G) Discernment:

www.TheologyofBusiness.com/GiftOfDiscernment

(H) Encouragement:

www.TheologyofBusiness.com/GiftOfEncouragement

(I) Evangelism:

www.TheologyofBusiness.com/GiftOfEvangelism

(J) Faith:

www.TheologyofBusiness.com/GiftOfFaith

(K) Giving:

www.TheologyofBusiness.com/GiftOfGiving

(L) Hospitality:

www.TheologyofBusiness.com/GiftOfHospitality

(M) Intercessory Prayer:

www.TheologyofBusiness.com/GiftOfIntercessoryPrayer

(N) Knowledge:

www.TheologyofBusiness.com/GiftOfKnowledge

(O) Leadership:

www.TheologyofBusiness.com/GiftOfLeadership

(P) Miracle-Working & Healing:

www.TheologyofBusiness.com/GiftsOfMiraclesAndHealing

(Q) Pastoring:

www.TheologyofBusiness.com/GiftOfPastoring

(R) Prophecy:

www.TheologyofBusiness.com/GiftOfProphecy

(S) Service:

www.TheologyofBusiness.com/GiftOfService

(T) Teaching:

www.TheologyofBusiness.com/GiftOfTeaching

(U) Tongues & Interpretation:

www.TheologyofBusiness.com/GiftsOfTonguesAndInterpretation

(V) Wisdom:

www.TheologyofBusiness.com/GiftOfWisdom

(W) Worship:

www.TheologyofBusiness.com/GiftOfWorship

ENDNOTES

1   "Our Story," Hobby Lobby website, https://newsroom.hobbylobby.
    com/corporate-background/.

2   "9 Things You Should Know About the Apostles' Creed," Joe Carter,
    The Gospel Coalition (TGC), December 12, 2018, https://www.
    thegospelcoalition.org/article/9-things-know-apostles-creed/.

3   "Top Ten Work Values Employers Look For," Penny Loretto,
    The Balance Careers, updated November 24, 2019, https://www.
    thebalancecareers.com/top-work-values-employers-look-for-1986763.

4   "Unlocking the Power of Prayer," Elizabeth Lombardo, *Success*,
    December 30, 2017, https://www.success.com/unlocking-the-power-
    of-prayer/.

5   "Mission & Vision Statements: What Is the Difference?" March
    5, 2018, Society for Human Resource Management, https://
    login.shrm.org/?request_id=id2D8D14DC02E599&relay_
    state=id-bc8b2c99-d3dc-49a0-9502-bc333a87915c&issuer=aH
    R0cHM6Ly9zc28uc2hybS5vcmcvSURCVVMvU0hTS9JRF
    AvU0FNTDIvTUQ=&target=aHR0cHM6Ly9zc28uc2hybS5v-
    cmcvSURCVVMvU0hTS9QT1JUQUwtU1AvU0FNTDIvTUQ=.

6   "Defining Company Culture: It's about Business Performance,
    Not Free Meals and Game Rooms," Natalie Baumgartner,
    Forbes, January 15, 2019, https://www.forbes.com/sites/

forbeshumanresourcescouncil/2019/01/15/defining-company-culture-its-about-business-performance-not-free-meals-and-game-rooms/#3024a1321e9d.

7   Ibid.

8   "Are You Emotionally Intelligent? Here's How to Know for Sure," Travis Bradberry, PhD, TalentSmart, https://www.talentsmart.com/articles/Are-You-Emotionally-Intelligent--Here%E2%80%99s-How-to-Know-for-Sure-2102500910-p-1.html.

9   "This Is Why You Should Speak Up about Work Problems," Nicole Lyn Pesce, MarketWatch, July 12, 2018, https://www.marketwatch.com/story/this-is-why-you-should-speak-up-about-work-problems-2018-07-12.

10 "Speaking Skills Top Employer Wish Lists. But Schools Don't Teach Them," Catherine Gewertz, *Education Week*, September 25, 2018, https://www.edweek.org/ew/articles/2018/09/26/speaking-skills-top-employer-wish-lists-but.html

11 "The Results Are Clear: Long Hours Backfire for People and for Companies," Sarah Green Carmichael, *Harvard Business Review*, August 19, 2015, https://hbr.org/2015/08/the-research-is-clear-long-hours-backfire-for-people-and-for-companies.

12 This assessment was created by Darren Shearer, founder of the Theology of Business Institute (www.TheologyofBusiness.com) and originally appeared in Darren's book, *The Marketplace Christian: A Practical Guide to Using Your Spiritual Gifts in Business*. © 2016 by Theology of Business. Reprinted with permission.

A free ebook edition is available with the purchase of this book.

To claim your free ebook edition:

Visit MorganJamesBOGO.com
Sign your name CLEARLY in the space
Complete the form and submit a photo of
the entire copyright page
You or your friend can download the ebook
to your preferred device

A **FREE** ebook edition is available for you
or a friend with the purchase of this print book.

CLEARLY SIGN YOUR NAME ABOVE

Instructions to claim your free ebook edition:
1. Visit MorganJamesBOGO.com
2. Sign your name CLEARLY in the space above
3. Complete the form and submit a photo
   of this entire page
4. You or your friend can download the ebook
   to your preferred device

Print & Digital Together Forever.

Snap a photo

Free ebook

Read anywhere

CPSIA information can be obtained
at www.ICGtesting.com
Printed in the USA
JSHW022223210721
17107JS00003B/245